MASTER
CONFLICT
WITHOUT
BEING A
B!T@H

Also by Dr. Judy Morley

5 Spiritual Steps to Overcome Adversity

The Leadership Constant

MASTER CONFLICT WITHOUT BEING A B!T@H

GET RESULTS
WITHOUT LOSING YOUR COOL

DR. JUDY MORLEY

MEDIA

Published 2023 by Gildan Media LLC
aka G&D Media
www.GandDmedia.com

FIRST EDITION 2023

Interior design by Meghan Day Healey of Story Horse, LLC

Library of Congress Cataloging-in-Publication Data is available upon request

ISBN: 978-1-7225-0627-8

10   9   8   7   6   5   4   3   2   1

CONTENTS

CONTENTS

1

THE ART OF CONFLICT

Let me guess. You hate conflict. You avoid it at all costs. To dodge it, you agree to do things you don't want to do. To deflect it, you lie to your significant other and say everything is "fine" when in fact you're upset. You stay mad at people for years rather than resolve the underlying issue because you don't want to create conflict.

Congratulations! You are completely normal. The problem is that while avoiding conflict makes you normal, it doesn't make you an effective friend, partner, community member, or, most importantly for the purposes of this book, leader.

Humans are hard-wired to fear conflict. When we lived in tribes, avoiding conflict was a survival mechanism. It's understandable to fear confrontation when the safety of the tribe is at stake. Humans have elaborate emotional systems to keep them safe, and fear is a vital part of those systems. The fight-or-flight response is the most common conflict avoidance mechanism, and it is triggered by any real or perceived threat.

Being hardwired to fear conflict, unfortunately, doesn't keep it from happening. The immediate threat may no longer be a fight with a saber-toothed tiger, but you are surrounded every day by potential conflict situations. From traffic altercations to family tension to workplace strife, day-to-day interactions are rife with opportunities for disagreements. As a matter of fact, differences of opinion are a hallmark of being human. Consequently, one of the most valuable skills a person—especially a leader—can learn is how to navigate conflict gracefully.

Leadership matters most when there is no agreement about how to move forward. Experts on leadership study war heroes because they led teams through stressful, rapidly changing circumstances. In these situations, everybody has an opinion, and no one seems to agree. The complications double if there is potential for conflict *within* the organization while facing external challenges. The most successful leaders navigate conflict without drama and confrontation.

I didn't fully appreciate the importance of gracefully handling conflict until I was in my early forties. For most of my life, I avoided conflict at all costs. Growing up in a dysfunctional, alcoholic household, I feared confrontation at a visceral level. Although I had had a successful career in multiple industries, I managed to succeed with "going along to get along," even if it weakened my results.

After years of exposure to corporate politics, I craved a calm and peaceful workplace. I decided to find a job where everyone got along. Ha! In my quest for a conflict-free workplace, I joined a spiritual nonprofit organization. I figured their peaceful, self-affirming philosophy ensured workplace harmony. When the nonprofit's headquarters moved to my hometown, I immediately got a job on the executive team. I loved that I could have my office filled with candles, om signs, peace symbols, and puffy cushions. I thought I'd finally found a workplace that would keep me free from conflict.

Was I in for a surprise! I learned firsthand that no matter how peaceful, lofty, and virtuous an organization's vision is, any company made up of humans has conflict. Within a few months, the organization announced it had serious financial challenges. Additionally, the move to a new office in a new city, with a completely new staff, led to confusion and upheaval on a grand scale. Finally, the company was in the process of merging with a group that had split from it fifty years earlier, so the process of coming back together reignited the contentious issues that had originally caused the separation.

I stayed in that position for seven years. When I left, the organization was financially prosperous, the move was a success, and the merger was complete. The greatest benefit for me, however, was that I got extremely comfortable with daily conflict. Since then, I've been fortunate to work with organizations, both for-profit and nonprofit, going through similar challenges. My clients have been predominantly women thrown into the midst of leadership dilemmas and feeling unprepared for them. I've consistently seen that leaders who can skillfully navigate conflict turn it into a creative, productive, and catalytic force. When conflict isn't handled well, it becomes toxic and destructive.

The most valuable lesson from these experiences was this: maneuvering conflict has less to do with circumstances than mindset. I can't find peace by trying to control the situation around me. Peace comes when I adjust my own attitude. Then I can be in the midst of conflict without being consumed by it. Handling conflict successfully starts with understanding personal beliefs, behaviors, triggers, and hot buttons. Once you're an expert on your internal emotional environment, you can effortlessly master conflict without being a bitch.

Why We Need Conflict . . .

Although it may seem counterintuitive, conflict is a necessary component of peaceful, successful organizations. In his classic book *The Five Dysfunctions of a Team*, author Patrick Lencioni cited a lack of conflict as a major dysfunction. Healthy teams need conflict to be proactive, creative, and productive. The same goes for healthy relationships, communities, and families. Healthy conflict isn't intense or threatening. It can be as benign as a small difference of opinion, but it's necessary for evolution. Without conflict, nothing grows.

Think about the most contentious situations you've faced. They may have been uncomfortable, even painful, experiences, but in hindsight you probably realized that they provided powerful wisdom and valuable lessons. The perspective of time shows that conflict was the very thing necessary to achieve greater success. There's a reason that every great movie, novel, or play has conflict at its heart. Without conflict, characters don't grow, life doesn't evolve, and no one cares.

In teams, conflict gives rise to better solutions. Challenges to a great idea reveal flaws and weaknesses that can be corrected along the way. Differing opinions enhance creativity and highlight new ways of problem-solving. Passionate disagreement gives birth to new perspectives. The wisdom of the group has magnifying power. One person may have an inspired *idea*, but it takes the entire group to come up with the inspired *solution*.

The jelly bean experiment illustrates the power of collective wisdom. At fairs and carnivals you've probably seen jars of jelly beans; participants guess how many are in the jar to win a prize. It's hard for an individual to guess the exact number of jelly beans. The answers vary widely, and the winning answer is usually as much as 10 percent off the actual number. However, in an experiment that has been repeated hundreds of times, statisticians have found that, if all the guesses are averaged together, the result is within 1 percent of the correct answer.*

---

* The original study was conducted in 1907 by statistician Francis Galton, who polled 800 fair attendees in Plymouth, England, asking them to guess the weight of an ox. He found that the median estimate was within .01 percent of the ox's weight. "The middlemost estimate expresses the *vox populi*," Galton noted. The experiment was repeated in 1987 by economist Jack Treynor, who found that in a smaller sampling, with only 56 people guessing the number of jellybeans in a jar, the median answer was less than 3 percent away from the actual number—better than any individual guess. These studies show that while individual guesses ranged dramatically, collective wisdom gave the most accurate measure.

While it would be lovely if every person in a group could cordially share their opinions to come to the collective wisdom, it rarely happens that way. Generally, ideas surface as two diametrically opposed viewpoints vying for ascendency, which creates conflict. It is up to you as the leader to navigate conflict, gain wisdom from all points of view, and maintain relationships to encourage a healthy team dynamic.

It all sounds very positive, doesn't it?

. . . And Why We Avoid Conflict

If conflict is key to healthy organizations, why do most people avoid it?

Let's face it: conflict is uncomfortable. It triggers deep emotions that feel destructive. Conflict also increases the likelihood of losing control, which compounds the discomfort. Nevertheless, there is a difference between a professional disagreement about next steps and a temper tantrum when you don't get your way. No one wants to indulge in the latter, but without skills, most people don't trust themselves to handle conflict appropriately.

Unfortunately, the twenty-first century hasn't been a banner time for learning about healthy conflict. Social media, polarization in mainstream news reporting, inflammatory rhetoric in political parties, generational strife in the workplace, and a lack of unifying leadership have made the first decades of the new millennium stressful and divided. There's plenty of conflict, but none of it resembles civil discourse. These unhealthy conflicts have "winners" and "losers," utilizing juvenile, bullying, and narcissistic behavior to force victory at all costs.

Clearly this is not healthy conflict.

The problematic nature of conflict comes from the human fear of losing control of emotions. Emotions are governed by the limbic brain, the oldest part of the brain, which is home to the fight-or-flight response. Because the limbic brain's job is to sense and avoid danger, it is reactionary, which puts it beyond your conscious awareness. When you take a comment personally, fear criticism, or feel insulted, the limbic brain triggers the fight-or-flight mechanism, creating an unhealthy reaction beyond your immediate control.

Luckily, humans also have a cerebral cortex, the outer layer of the brain, which governs reasoning, language, and decision making. The thought processes in the cerebral cortex defuse emotional reactions in the limbic brain, but they take longer to engage. If you've ever been so angry that you couldn't think of anything to say, only to come up with the perfect comeback once the confrontation was over, you have experienced the lag between the limbic brain and the cerebral cortex.

Discomfort with conflict stems from concern that the limbic brain will react before the cerebral cortex kicks in. Most people don't trust themselves to maintain composure in the face of potential conflict. If no one taught you about the interplay between the two parts of your brain, conflict feels like an emotional minefield—but it doesn't have to be. By recognizing your emotions and allowing your thought processes to govern them, you can work with, rather than be consumed by, the fight-or-flight response.

Cultural patterns compound the dread of conflict. You probably learned as a child that talking back, disagreeing, or asserting your opinion got you into trouble. Enforcing meekness in kids may make for a quiet household, but it doesn't create grownups who can handle conflict productively. Although the "children-should-be-seen-and-not-heard" method of parenting has gone out of style, kids still get the message: don't argue, don't contradict, don't create a fuss. Once grown up, many flat out rebel. Surely you remember your teenage years! It may be liberating to rebel instead of repressing emotions, but that isn't productive either. The repression-rebellion cycle, common in both personal and professional situations, exacerbates the fear and taboo around conflict.

You've probably also experienced the close relationship between anger and conflict. It's easier to disagree when you feel justified by anger. It's human nature to blame first and ask questions later. Unresolved anger simmering below the surface on both sides of tense interactions creates a vicious cycle that prolongs interpersonal strife. Allowing conflict to be processed as soon as it arises breaks the cycle.

One key to separating anger from conflict is to have an abiding faith in positive outcomes. It may sound Pollyannaish, but life always evolves forward. I have witnessed it time after time. I believe the quote attributed to John Lennon, which says, "Everything will be OK in the end. If it's not OK, it's not the end." Although this may be hard to believe at any given moment, with hindsight it becomes obvious that everything happens for a reason, and conflict is always a catalyst.

Healthy Conflict versus Antagonism

Since all conflict triggers fear, it's difficult to separate healthy conflict from antagonism, but there is a huge difference between them. Healthy conflict, as I've suggested, is a necessary factor of growth. Differences of opinion are prevalent in every human institution. Even identical twins don't agree on everything all the time. Healthy conflict leads to the free interchange of ideas; ultimately, it is a benefit to a relationship, team, or project.

Antagonism is a different dynamic altogether. Antagonism stems from a person who is compelled to disagree, regardless of the context or consequences. Antagonists aren't seeking resolution; they only want power and attention. They grab influence by challenging the leader through contradictory behavior. Antagonists take a position in favor of something one week and against something similar the next week, just to protest authority. They waste time and energy trying to manipulate outcomes.

Antagonists never learn to be team players. They aren't interested in helping the organization: they're only interested in their own standing within the team. When there is a disagreement, antagonists go to great lengths to prove themselves right and won't apologize or accept any compromise.

It can be tricky and time-consuming to determine whether someone is an antagonist or just passionate about their opinion. The biggest identifier of antagonists is that it is impossible to find a solution that satisfies them. A team player is willing to consider and reconsider options, but an antagonist never does.

Frequently, it seems that everyone is an antagonist. When there is wide-scale disagreement, particularly when the same people disagree all the time, it's tempting to brand them as antagonists, but that isn't necessarily the case. Just because someone disagrees about several issues does not make that person an antagonist. Although it's crucial to weed out antagonists, you should also be careful about surrounding yourself with yes-people.

In short, an antagonist thrives on being an antagonist. He or she will take a contrary position regardless of the topic. By contrast, team members trying to work within the boundaries of healthy conflict are solution-oriented. They don't necessarily want to argue and will keep trying to find an answer. Antagonists thrive on conflict. Any solution threatens the antagonist's identity. When a solution is proposed, an antagonist will fight it every time.

You will probably meet a few antagonists in your career. It is crucial to identify and eliminate them. They will always prolong conflict and make it unhealthy and personal, and that's exactly what you want to avoid. Use your authority to remove them quickly from their position.

Pitfalls of Going Along to Get Along
The opposite of an antagonist is someone who goes along to get along. At first, it might not seem so bad

to have a people-pleaser on your team, especially if you've dealt with an antagonist. After all, the pleaser probably won't instigate conflict, at least not overtly. Nonetheless, a people-pleaser can be every bit as detrimental as an antagonist. People-pleasers crave approval. They love every idea you have and agree with every initiative you offer. Although this might seem like heaven, it doesn't last.

No person can genuinely love everything you do. Consequently, the people-pleaser seems enthusiastic in front of you but undermines your decisions later. It turns into passive-aggressive behavior: the pleaser appears to agree in front of the team but bad-mouths the decision at the water cooler. In many ways, this person is more dangerous to your team than an antagonist, because the conflict is not out in the open, where you can handle it. It is hidden under layers of mixed messages, which makes it harder to find and address.

What if *you* are the people-pleaser? Many women have found this to be an effective strategy for getting into leadership, particularly in male-dominated industries. The problem with going along to get along is that once you're the person making decisions, you only have two choices about how to manage your team: be everyone's friend or a total bitch. Neither choice makes for good leadership. There is a third option, however, and that is what this book is all about.

Why Women Need This Most

Historically, women were taught to avoid conflict more than men. The things that foster conflict—competition, argument, confrontation, and aggression—are all more acceptable in a male-dominated environment. Women get the message that it's not ladylike to argue or stand up for oneself: hence going along to get along. Females are socialized to be kind, nurturing, and understanding, regardless of someone else's bad behavior. For nurturers and caregivers, conflict becomes difficult to reconcile. Frequently, little girls are chastised for getting mad and told that it's not feminine to be angry. Women frequently express anger through tears, which are inappropriate in professional settings. Because conflict runs contrary to the socialized ideal of womanhood, women learn that conflict makes them unfeminine or, frankly, bitches.

Although powerful women have existed throughout history, the current paradigm for female leaders comes from post–World War II corporate America. During the war, women entered the workforce in unprecedented numbers. They served as nurses and support staff in the military, worked in factories,

built airplanes and ships, and entered service industries vacated by men going to fight the war. Rosie the
Riveter became iconic, but she didn't permanently
change expectations for women.

Although women had more doors open to them in
the postwar period, the ensuing flight to the suburbs
and beginning of the baby boom undermined Rosie
the Riveter and replaced her with June Cleaver—the
mild-mannered parent who couldn't even discipline
her own children without her husband ("Just wait
until your father gets home!"). The image of Mother
as the softie and Father as the disciplinarian ran
through popular culture and affected gender roles in
industry as well.

While Rosie was giving way to June, American
corporate structure took on its twentieth-century
identity. Soldiers returned from war and got college educations on the GI Bill. They entered the
white-collar workforce in unprecedented numbers.
Corporate America remained a male-dominated
world, and women opted to stay in their new subur-
ban homes and raise the passel of children they had.

By the time of the women's liberation movement
in the 1970s, postwar patterns were firmly established. Women who attained leadership roles adapted
their personalities and management styles to a male-
dominated paradigm. This left female leaders with

the choice of acting like men or being doormats. When women didn't stand up for themselves, their careers suffered; their ideas weren't valued, they didn't get the recognition they deserved, and they failed to advance. To rectify this pattern, women acted more like men. But this approach earned women the reputation of being "bitches," which meant being unfeminine, unattractive, and unapproachable.

As unfair as these prejudgments are, they happen. Whether they *should* happen or not is irrelevant, because as long as society operates this way, these opinions affect female leaders. Prejudgments take place all the time, and it's more effective to navigate them rather than resist them. The good news is that there is a way to be an effective leader without having to be either a doormat or a bitch.

The nurturing traits conditioned into women have become increasingly important in the professional world. As businesses become more relationship-oriented than ever, the female knack for relationship building is increasingly highly valued. The very thing that, in the past, women tried to overcome is now an asset to their careers.

At the same time, the missing piece for women in nurturing relationships is navigating conflict. Identifying productive conflict and effectively dealing with it are skills toward which women still don't gravitate. When disagreement threatens the female role as peacekeeper, the ensuing conflict triggers anger, which quickly turns unproductive and leads women to be bitches.

Let me talk about the word *bitch*. For some reason, this word is a favorite epithet thrown at women who fail to go along to get along. It has become a loaded insult for many women. When I first started writing this book, most people loved the title—especially men. However, one dear friend was really upset by the name. She cautioned me that if I used the word *bitch* in the title, I would turn away a lot of readers. Another friend won't even use the word. Whenever she refers to this book, she calls it the book about "being a witch with a B."

This led me to do a little informal market research. I found that there is a generational difference of opinion among women about the word *bitch*. In my unscientific, informal survey, I found that for baby boomers and Gen Xers, the word has a very negative connotation. Most of these women feel it's the ultimate sexist insult and avoid using it so they aren't guilty of committing the same transgression.

As with so many other things, however, millennials redefined the term. They have taken control of the word by embracing it and using it ironically. They now have bumper stickers that tell them to "embrace your inner bitch" and find inner peace with the words, "Namaste, bitches!" As with other offensive labels of the 1960s and '70s, this younger generation is taking the power out of it by reassigning meaning and embracing it as their own.

In this context, I have consciously used the b-word. When it comes to dealing with conflict, women must stop fearing what others think and start doing things that move their businesses, teams, and careers forward. There is a huge difference between being clear, direct, and no-nonsense and being a bitch. If someone misinterprets good leadership behaviors for bitchiness, it is time for females to stop caring. This doesn't give women carte blanche to be unpleasant or cruel, but it does give them the freedom—and the responsibility—to learn how to manage conflict in productive ways without getting caught up in the possible consequences.

What You'll Get Out of This Book

The topics and techniques covered in this book are meant to be used in professional situations where there is a power differential—for example, where you are the leader of a team. But many of these techniques also work in your community, family, or church.

The idea for this book came from a conversation with my personal coach. I was struggling with how I could best help my clients, many of whom are women. I was wrestling with the types of classes I could provide, the transformation I wanted to lead my clients through, and what I really contributed to the lives of women in leadership. As I fumbled to find words to describe my passion, my coach kept pressing me to clarify. I got more and more frustrated, until finally I blurted out, "I just want these women leaders to know they can handle conflict without having to be a bitch!"

Everything stopped. My coach looked at me and said, "That's it. That's what you do." She was right. That's what I've been doing my entire career, whether I knew it or not. I have helped leaders overcome adversity, navigate change, and manage difficult relationships for over twenty years. I've called it other things, but all of it revolved around mastering personal and professional conflict.

Over the past two decades, I've had plenty of opportunities to lead clients, teams, and organizations through situations that were rife with conflict. Whether it was dealing with personal adversity, such as a serious health crisis, a divorce, a bankruptcy, a life trauma, or an organizational conflict (like a reorganization, home office relocation, acquisition, or merger), the common denominator was always learning how to deal with conflict productively.

I have taken all I've learned and boiled it down to five strategies. If you've read my previous books, you'll find that I like the number five. Five strategies are comprehensive enough to cover everything, but easy enough to remember. Because most conflict arises from unhealed personal emotions and sloppy communication skills, the bulk of the techniques in this book are personal growth and self-expression strategies. When you first read these concepts, they seem basic. However, it's not the theory behind them that makes them powerful. The punch comes from daily practice and implementing them in every human interaction you have.

Each chapter begins with the internal shift you need to make to handle conflict more effectively. It's crucial to examine your own beliefs, habits, and feelings about conflict. Some people experience paralyzing fear or uncontrollable anger in the midst of conflict, and it's critical to recognize that. Each chapter asks you to identify and shift your beliefs about a certain aspect of conflict so you can be more effective. These are "being" changes.

The next part of each chapter provides ideas and tactics to use with your team. I have addressed the most common areas of potential conflict and provided tips and tactics. You may already know some of them, but the power comes in making them second nature. These are "doing" changes. Each chapter ends with a list of five mindset shifts to implement and five new habits to practice.

In each chapter, I provide a historical example of a woman who handled conflict without being a bitch. I use historical illustrations because I believe they provide clear examples of leadership in a context where the outcome is well established. I've also included contemporary cases from my clients and experiences. I have used all of the contemporary stories with permission, although I changed the names for privacy purposes.

Although I sometimes call the concepts in this book "steps," they aren't necessarily sequential. Some build on one another, but many of them overlap. Depending on your situation, you may take part of one step and combine it with part of another. Mastering them all gives you a full set of tools to use when conflict arises.

This book isn't about your team, staff, or colleagues. It's about YOU. If you have the discipline to master these five strategies, you will be much more confident in situations with potential conflict. You will no longer fear conflict, so you won't worry about interactions that might start it. You can enter every situation, relationship, or conversation with the bedrock ability to stand up for yourself, listen thoroughly to the other person's perspective, and avoid bruised egos or hurt feelings. Ultimately, you'll have the confidence to get results.

It is my deepest desire for you as a leader to never worry about being called the b-word again. You can be direct, you can be clear, you can be forceful, and you can be kind through all of it. In short, you will be able to master conflict absolutely without being a bitch.

But most of all, if someone does call you a bitch, I want you to walk away with enough confidence not to care.

2

ANTICIPATE POTENTIAL PROBLEMS

As the old adage says, "The best defense is a good offense." Managing conflict entails preparing before it happens. Most leaders know the areas in their organization that are prone to conflict. They vary from industry to industry, but every industry has them. They are generally areas that require a high level of interdependence between individuals and teams. Anticipating potential problems gives you time to defuse conflict before it starts.

It takes the proper mindset to look at a situation and anticipate problems. As an eternal optimist, I had to work at this: I felt negative when anticipating problems. I realized, however, that anticipating a problem isn't the same as creating a problem, or even hoping for one. No one can manage what isn't addressed. Being prepared for anything dissolves nervousness about possible confrontations, allowing for creativity and peace. By anticipating potential problems, you can avoid them without having to be a bitch.

Build Emotional Awareness

As with most things, anticipating potential problems starts with you. Before you can accurately identify what's happening around you, you must be aware of your mental, physical, and emotional states. Humans are a complex jumble of feelings, and it takes emotional intelligence (EQ) to navigate interactions and relationships. Over the past twenty years, EQ became a buzzword in leadership circles. It's claimed to be a greater indicator of success than intellect. Unlike intellectual intelligence (IQ), which is supposedly set at birth, EQ is a skill and can be learned. Like all skills, it takes practice and awareness. However, understanding and managing emotions—both yours and those of the people around you—pays huge dividends.

Unfortunately, emotional intelligence isn't taught in school. Most of what is passed on about emotions comes from family, teachers, and the media, which aren't great emotional role models. The majority of people can't identify what they're feeling in any given moment, let alone understand the twisting emotional path that brought them to that feeling. It's usually easier to identify emotional triggers in another person than it is in yourself.

Nonetheless, understanding the nature of conflict means looking in the mirror. It may be convenient to believe that bad behavior starts with everyone else, but that's generally not true. Becoming a leader suddenly requires you to take a crash course in emotional intelligence. To set a good example, you don't have the luxury of remaining emotionally unaware. Realize you have hidden beliefs that cause you to overreact, withdraw, or harbor resentment. The more you know about your emotional states, the better prepared you are to identify problems before they begin.

You probably weren't taught a lot about emotions as a child. If you're like most people, you mainly learned to avoid them. Well-meaning authority figures weren't necessarily trying to handicap you. They were repeating the pattern they learned. If their parents never taught them to understand emotions, they weren't equipped to teach you either. The pattern may go back generations. Even so, mastering conflict requires you to break the pattern and become a self-taught expert on emotions.

The Four Basic Competencies

Emotional intelligence consists of four basic competencies. Two of them address the awareness and
management of your own emotions, and two address
the awareness and management of other people's
emotions.

The first component of emotional intelligence is
self-awareness. You can't be emotionally in tune with
what's happening around you if you aren't aware of
your own feelings. Self-awareness sounds straightforward, but it's not as easy as it sounds. How many
times have you said you were "fine" when you really
weren't, shaken off an infuriating encounter, believing it made you the bigger person, or choked back
tears and pretended to have something in your eye?
Over time, denying your emotions conditions you
to disconnect from them until you don't know what
you're feeling.

The best way to build self-awareness is to listen
to your body. Your mind lies. The intellect will convince you that you aren't feeling something, but your
body will always tell the truth. For example, watch
what happens to your breathing when you get angry.
Your mind may tell you that you aren't really mad,
but your respiration speeds up regardless. When you
are sad, your throat tightens, lips quiver, eyes water,

and nose runs even as you struggle to maintain control. Fear increases your heart rate, as adrenaline and cortisol pump into your system from the fight-or-flight response, even if you rationally understand you aren't in danger.

Paying attention to your body's cues brings attention to old emotional patterns. If you are sitting at your desk on a Tuesday afternoon and suddenly your heart starts pounding and your breathing gets heavy, ask yourself what you were thinking about that triggered this reaction. You may realize that a tense encounter with a team member reminded you of an old conflict from years ago. You may be dreading making a presentation to the board in the morning. Whatever triggered them, unprocessed emotions have unexpectedly resurged. Thanks to your body, you are now aware of them.

Once you are adept at self-awareness, the next step in building EQ is *self-management.* You may have learned it's inappropriate to reveal your emotions, so you've equated *showing* them with *feeling* them. *It's never inappropriate to feel what you feel.* The key is how you manage your response. Pretending you don't have emotions, or stuffing them, is more destructive than feeling them. Unexpressed anger and sadness have been linked to chronic depression, anxiety, cancer, heart disease, and high blood pressure. Refusing to feel your emotions is not an option. Learning to manage them, however, builds EQ.

Self-management is, first and foremost, a mindset. It's frightening to be hijacked by your emotions, unable to control your behavior. Controlling your mindset stops this hijacking. Thoughts create emotions, and when you reframe your thoughts, your emotions settle. If you notice your heart racing, palms sweating, or jaw clenched, watch how your thoughts are influencing the physical symptoms. Notice the correlation between what you were thinking and how you felt. When you identify the triggering thought, try thinking about something completely unrelated. For example, if you were worried about finances the moment before you got anxious, try thinking about eating ice cream, going skiing, or having a movie night. Notice how interrupting the thought mitigates the feelings.

Your body can also shift emotions. Relax the muscles in your jaw. Shake your hands and arms until your palms are no longer clammy. The old technique of counting to ten before getting angry gives your rational mind—the cerebral cortex—time to catch up with your emotional, limbic brain, which just reacts. This technique allows the adrenaline and cortisol coursing through your body to subside before you react in a way you may regret. Use your body as a self-management tool, and consciously choose a response instead of reacting without thinking.

Learning self-awareness and self-management is crucial to mastering conflict. I worked with a manager who had no self-awareness or self-management skills. If something made him happy, he congratulated and rewarded the whole team. However, if something made him angry—whether it had anything to do with work or not—he turned into a tyrant who inflicted his temper tantrums on the team. He never apologized, causing simmering anger and resentment throughout the office. It left everyone walking on eggshells, which undermined trust and inhibited communication. Conflict abounded, and he was the epicenter. Ultimately, the business failed.

Once you're adept at your own emotions, expand to understand other people's. The third EQ skill is *social awareness*, which entails reading and interpreting cues to other people's emotional states. As we've already seen, no one can really hide what they feel for long, because the body tattles.

In the 1970s, Dr. Albert Mehrabian, a professor at UCLA, did a study regarding communication about emotions. He suggested that only 7 percent of meaning is communicated through the spoken word, while 38 percent takes place through tone of voice and the remaining 55 percent takes place through body language. Although this study has been casually cited as decisive for all communication, Dr. Mehrabian was specifically studying how people talk about feelings. He concluded that 93 percent of emotional communication happens from nonverbal cues. Learning to read them increases social awareness.

Empathy is the foundation of social awareness. Understanding someone else's emotional state without judgment is a rare and supportive skill. Empathy requires more than putting yourself in another person's shoes: it also demands stepping into the other person's worldview. Leaders have different perspectives than their team members. What seems like a sound management decision to you might come across as a demotion, punishment, or retaliation to someone on your staff. If you take time to think about your decisions from a different perspective and imagine how they make other people feel, you can change your communication strategy and avoid drama.

Relationship Management

The final component of emotional intelligence is *relationship management*. This skill requires defining each person's role in a relationship and managing accordingly. Relationship management doesn't mean micromanaging interactions between people. It requires keeping everyone focused on common goals for a project. Once these goals are established, team members don't have to like one another. They just have to work together to achieve the desired outcome. Don't try to make them into friends. Just be sure they get the job done. For example, if you are the chairperson of a nonprofit board, you might have two members who disagree on just about every aspect of life. However, if these two members are cochairing the annual fundraiser, you only have to manage their relationship for that event. If they remain focused on the task, committed to the vision for the project, and enthusiastic about the event, they don't need to be BFFs.

Relationship management is one of the trickiest aspects of emotional intelligence, because so much is out of your control. With the first three EQ competencies, you can build skills and learn techniques to perfect them. With relationship management, sometimes the other people just won't cooperate! But if you are skilled in the other three, you can navigate relationship management. The combination of the four skills enables you to anticipate potential problems between team members and respond appropriately.

Don't Take Anything Personally

A hallmark of emotional intelligence is learning to never take anything personally. It sounds simple, right? It's easy to understand, but harder to do. The limbic brain jumps to conclusions, gets defensive, and reacts in anger before the cerebral cortex even knows there's a problem. It's easy to believe a comment is directed at you when most likely it's not. If you have strong self-awareness, you're less likely to take things personally. Being realistic about your abilities makes you less likely to become offended or defensive. No one is perfect.

If you start to take something personally, pause for a reality check. Let the cerebral cortex catch up. Take deep breaths. Force yourself to broaden your perspective and look at the situation from several different angles. Ask clarifying questions, if appropriate. These actions take less than two minutes and help you identify whether you were looking at the situation realistically or you were allowing a subconscious filter to skew the truth. When you stop taking anything personally, you can brainstorm with your team, admit your shortcomings, and laugh at your mistakes in public. Taking things personally wastes time and energy trying to examine what you did "wrong" and defending your actions. If you channel that energy into creative solutions, there's less like-lihood of conflict.

One way to stop taking things personally is to identify your triggers—specific situations that cause an intense emotional reaction disproportionate to the circumstances. Humans have emotional baggage from the past, and triggers bring those past events into the present in inappropriate ways. Emotionally intelligent leaders recognize triggers and know how to navigate them. If you don't know about a sub-conscious trigger until someone sets it off, you've probably already created conflict.

Triggers are difficult to identify in yourself, but ridiculously easy to see in other people. When some-one overreacts, it is probably a trigger. If you witness team members arguing over inconsequential facts, it is a trigger. If you walk onstage at the Academy Awards and slap someone for poking fun at your wife, it's certainly the result of some childhood bag-gage that was never resolved—the definition of a trigger.

Triggers powerfully dictate behavior. Years ago, I struggled to get along with a particular employee. No matter what I did or said, he got defensive. No matter how much I praised his work, he complained that I didn't appreciate him. Whenever I asked him for infor-mation, it took days, if not weeks, to get a response.

The relationship got so bad that I finally had to take disciplinary action. The meeting did not go well, and I was completely prepared for him to quit the next day.

Consequently, I wasn't surprised when I arrived the next morning to find an email from him, asking to meet with me. I expected him to submit his resignation, and I prepared myself for it. I wasn't going to react, just accept the resignation and start the hiring process.

To my surprise—and his credit—that didn't happen. During our meeting, he explained that I reminded him of his mother, with whom he had an incredibly dysfunctional relationship. Everything about me was a trigger. Whatever I said sounded like criticism because he projected his relationship with his mom onto me.

Identifying his trigger took great self-awareness on his part, as well as courage. He apologized for his behavior and asked that we have regular meetings to continue building our relationship. He ended up being a great staff member, and we rarely had a conflict after those initial incidents.

The nature of conflict is rarely what it seems to be. When you understand that people regularly react from triggers, you realize that 99 percent of conflict isn't about the issue at hand, but about old emotional patterns. Consequently, it's critical to avoid taking anything personally. Building emotional intelligence skills helps you achieve that.

Establish Agreements

Potential conflict among team members generally stems from broken agreements. There are multiple spoken and unspoken agreements in the workplace, and conflict happens when these agreements aren't honored. The more explicitly you state these agreements, the easier they are to maintain.

Agreements take buy-in and ground rules. Establishing agreements creates explicit social contracts to prevent problems down the road. To build team agreements, first establish shared values. Most of your team members have opinions about what they are doing and how it should be done. Differences of opinion are potential conflict areas. When you peel back the opinions, however, people working together can find common ground with shared values. Build agreements around values, and go toward your goals from there. Tie everything to values. Don't let the team forget that regardless of differences of opinion, they all want the same thing.

After articulating shared values, assess the level of trust in your organization. According to Queen's University in Toronto, Ontario, there are three types of trust: *governance- and rules-based trust*; *experi-ence- and confidence-based trust*; *established and vulnerability-based trust.* These three categories determine how effective your agreements are and where they might break down.

Governance- and rules-based trust is the most basic level of trust. It includes things like believ-ing that a colleague will follow the law, policies, procedures, and contracts. You trust them to keep agreements. In a relationship at this level, you count on the other person to follow the rules that govern your behavior with one another. Conflict at work fre-quently stems from a violation of this kind of trust, as when an employee perceives that someone is breaking the rules. Whether they tell a supervisor or quietly resent it, the breakdown in trust is an oppor-tunity for conflict.

The second level of trust is *experience- and confidence-based trust.* Whereas the first level of trust depends on confidence in a colleague's actions, the second level has to do with his or her intentions. At this level, you have experience with the other per-son, share values, and accept that the person is acting with integrity. This level of trust rests on shared experience and prior positive interactions. In new sit-uations or inexperienced teams, a lack of this type of trust could cause conflict.

The deepest level of trust is *established and vulnerability trust*, which is rarer in the workplace, since it's usually reserved for intimate connections. As its name suggests, this form of trust is built over time. At this level, you know the other person's dreams, goals, and fears. You are willing to share your deepest beliefs and have faith that this knowledge will never be misused. Trust flows easily between both parties in all situations.

Understanding the three levels of trust allows you to assess the effectiveness of agreements. As you observe the level of trust between team members, you can anticipate where broken agreements might arise. The absence of rules-based trust will breed suspicion at the most basic level. A lack of confidence-based trust means teams without a track record are more likely to break agreements. Recognizing the trust levels makes it easier to evaluate possible breakdowns at either of these levels and take corrective action before problems arise.

Assessing trust requires active listening. Active listening is a specialized skill requiring paying close attention to what's happening among your team members. In general, people define "listening" as "waiting to speak." When they hear something that matches their own ideas, they take the other person's comments as agreement with their point of view, whether that's true or not. The danger of this confirmation bias is that it keeps leaders from hearing what's really happening. It only reinforces what they already think. It's hard to find potential problems while living in denial.

Active listening involves focusing intently on what the other person is saying. If you have asked questions about a project, have the courtesy to listen actively to the reply. To ensure you're following along, repeat back what the other person told you. Say things like, "If I heard you correctly, what you're saying is . . ." or "Just so I understand, you're telling me that . . ." Active listening helps overcome confirmation bias. Sometimes what you hear might not be comfortable, but allowing yourself to stay with the discomfort highlights communication breakdowns and provides early warning signs of relationship tension.

A great technique that helps with both assessing trust and active listening is convening a *premortem* session. You've no doubt heard of a postmortem, which is a medical term for determining the cause of death in a patient. A premortem is an evaluation of a project before it begins in order to determine the cause of potential failure. Organizations started using the process to anticipate problems before they started.

A premortem consists of calling all stakeholders together to talk through the project, step-by-step, before it begins. The session provides an opportunity for team members to have input into each phase and dissect all possible outcomes—positive and negative. It can help pinpoint possible breakdowns in trust, unspoken agendas, ideas that hadn't previously been heard, and bottlenecks in the process. The meeting identifies conflicts of interest or personality clashes before the project goes too far. It allows the team to build agreements that avoid pitfalls and highlight areas that could cause delays and conflict later.

You can use the premortem at all levels of your organization. You don't need to be involved in every premortem meeting. Different teams can implement them. Subteams or small groups can use them with great success. Establishing premortems as part of your culture helps your team make agreements to fit the goal. Intermittent premortems allow you to adjust project specifications and guidelines to meet deadlines and budgets as well as anticipate potential problems.

Benchmarks

Once you've established agreements, set frequent benchmarks. Setting benchmarks reminds me of the old question, "How do you eat an elephant?" The answer, of course, is, "One bite at a time." It's daunting to understand an entire project. For someone at a lower level of the organization, who isn't privy to the big picture, benchmarks create manageable goals to keep progress moving.

Setting benchmarks allows you to quickly catch misunderstandings or poor performance. You're able to identify interpersonal conflict or a breakdown in trust at each benchmark. Checking in at benchmark meetings accommodates active listening, while missing a benchmark deadline provides time for a course correction before it derails the whole project. Benchmark meetings can act as premortems for the next stage.

If your team has established strong agreements and maintains frequent benchmarks, the only thing for you to practice is managing behaviors, not opinions. When geared to anticipate conflict, it's easy to tune into people who don't agree with each other. Understandably, differences of opinion can lead to conflict, but they don't have to if you manage behavior wisely. Not everyone on your team will agree, and they may all have different ideas about how a project should be done, but as long as their behavior is professional and the project gets done, you don't have an issue. Pick your battles so you don't create unnecessary conflict. Sometimes people just don't agree, and this doesn't have to be a problem.

It's hard to distinguish between behaviors and attitudes, especially if you believe a team member is undermining you. It's helpful to step back and do a reality check. Insubordination is a behavior you can manage, but a good employee in a bad mood isn't necessarily an actionable item. Having a bad day or being cranky isn't a reason to take an employee off the project, but someone sabotaging it, stalling progress, or being an antagonist is. Make sure that a person's conduct isn't just something you don't like but an actual behavior that's detrimental to the team, project, or organization.

You don't need, or want, a workforce that walks together in lockstep harmony. Civil disagreement is fruitful and productive, if you accept it without trying to make everyone get along. The people on your team have different political views, religious traditions, and educational biases. As long as they work together toward the common goal and don't let it spill over onto the rest of the team, graciously accept disagreement, and focus only on managing behavior.

Sacagawea's Leadership

Someone I admire for her ability to anticipate and navigate potential conflict was Sacagawea, who guided the Lewis and Clark Expedition from 1804 to 1806.

In 1803, President Thomas Jefferson commissioned Meriwether Lewis and William Clark to explore the Louisiana Territory, newly purchased from France. No one was sure exactly what Jefferson had bought, and there were rumors of a Northwest Passage to Asia through the North American continent. Lewis's and Clark's expedition, also known as the Corps of Discovery, left St. Charles, Missouri, in 1804 to map the territory. They traveled up the Missouri River to Fort Mandan, in present-day North Dakota, for the winter of 1804–05.

Here they met young Sacagawea. Born a Lemhi Shoshone, Sacagawea was kidnapped by the Hidatsa tribe in 1800, at approximately twelve years old. The next year, the Hidatsas sold her into a nonconsensual marriage to a French-Canadian fur trapper named Toussaint Charbonneau. Charbonneau and his young wife wintered with the Hidatsas at Fort Mandan, where they met the Corps of Discovery. Charbonneau informed expedition leaders that his wife was a "Snake" (Shoshone) Indian and spoke the language of the people whose territory they were about to enter. He offered her as an interpreter and guide. At the time, Sacagawea was pregnant.

Talk about anticipating potential conflict! At approximately seventeen years old, Sacagawea found herself at the intersection of multiple conflicting cultures. It was her responsibility to ensure safe passage for the Corps of Discovery through territory belonging to almost twenty-five Native American nations. She also guided the corps through the dangerous terrain of Lemhi Pass, where she was born. She did it all with raging pregnancy and postpartum hormones. Sacagawea faced the same dangers as the men in the Corps of Discovery while carrying an infant on her back.

Given her tumultuous early life, Sacagawea had clearly developed emotional intelligence to survive in captivity. According to accounts from the men in the corps, she had excellent self-awareness and self-management skills. She was naturally reserved, but unlike her husband, was able to express herself calmly and clearly. She worked with William Clark to establish agreements among the men for the safety of the passage. She assessed the trust among the members of the Corps of Discovery, between members of the corps and her husband, and between the entire expedition and the various tribes they encountered. Her very presence helped build trust, because in the warrior culture of early nineteenth-century Plains Indians, no war party would travel with a woman and infant. Her presence signaled peace.

Sacagawea was an astute observer and actively listened when the soldiers got nervous or frightened.

Although she spoke neither French nor English, she used her ability to read body language and tonality to "listen" to plans. She recognized that their fear could jeopardize the expedition and taught them survival skills. For example, when food ran low, she showed them how to cook and eat camas roots to regain their strength. She played a critical role in planning each step of the expedition, something unheard of for a woman in the nineteenth century, especially a native woman. She inserted herself into the planning process to make recommendations, in a primitive version of a premortem. Her knowledge of the terrain and weather set benchmarks for the expedition to maintain progress, so they didn't get caught in the high Rockies during the winter.

Sacagawea's leadership was so valuable that even William Clark deferred to her judgment. With her skills at anticipating conflict, she steered the Corps of Discovery to avoid confrontations both within the organization (by helping keep peace among the men) and outside the organization (with multiple Indian tribes). Although the party failed to find a Northwest Passage, Sacagawea guided the expedition over the Continental Divide to the Snake River. From there, she led them down the Columbia River to the Pacific Ocean, where they wintered at Fort Clatsop in relative safety.

Sacagawea and Charbonneau returned to live among the Hidatsas after the expedition, but accepted William Clark's invitation to join him in St. Louis in 1809. Clark had grown fond of Sacagawea's son, Jean Baptiste Charbonneau, who accompanied them on the expedition, and offered to raise him as his own. In 1812, Sacagawea gave birth to a daughter, Lizette, but Clark does not mention her after her birth, and historians believe she died as an infant. Sacagawea passed away that same year at Fort Mandan, approximately twenty-five years old. Despite barriers of language, culture, and gender, her ability to anticipate potential problems and find solutions made the Lewis and Clark Expedition the most peaceful of all westward expeditions.

Merging Organizations

Two hundred years later, I had the privilege to work with another woman leader, Deborah, who exhibited a similar ability to anticipate and avoid potential problems.

Deborah was a marketing executive in the midst of rebranding a large membership organization with diverse stakeholders. The old brand image dated to the organization's founder, who had introduced it eighty years earlier. Many factions of the organization wanted to grow, and they knew the outdated image wasn't appealing to a younger generation.

The organization hired Deborah to oversee market research and create a new brand identity to facilitate growth. Like Sacagawea, Deborah led them on a metaphorical expedition into the unknown. Deborah's goals were to develop a new corporate identity, including a name change, new logo, and updated imagery. Although the test group of target audience members loved Deborah's work, the established members were unwilling to leave behind the old brand. The process was complicated by the fact that different subsets of the membership objected to different aspects of the new brand, with some embracing the name change but not the logo, others embracing the imagery but not the name change, and others rejecting all of it.

First, Deborah made sure she didn't bring any of her own conflict to the project. She practiced her emotional intelligence skills. She recognized that the organization was inherently divided and prepared herself to get caught in the middle. She constantly reminded herself not to take anything personally.

Although the task was not quite as fraught as Sacagawea's expedition through uncharted native territory, Deborah quickly found that she could avoid potential conflict between warring "tribes" in the organization by assessing trust and actively listening.

She realized the disagreements had little to do with the brand and stemmed from a historic breakdown in experience- and confidence-based trust. She shifted gears away from marketing and actively listened to the different factions, carefully ascertaining how much of their dislike of the brand had to do with the actual package and how much had to do with their lack of trust. She found that a plethora of misunderstandings dated back decades.

Once she determined what was really happening, Deborah assembled representatives from all the stakeholders within the membership to establish agreements about outcomes and processes. She called a premortem meeting. She asked stakeholders to explain what they thought would happen if each of their pet scenarios was implemented. What if they changed the name but kept the old logo? What if they changed everything? What if they changed nothing? Through this process, the stakeholders realized their only options were to change nothing and remain stagnant or change everything and grow. They came to consensus without a major conflict.

Once she'd established the agreement, Deborah set frequent benchmarks. With every step in the design process, she held a stakeholders' meeting to get feedback and be sure everyone was making progress. She established a rollout plan so each group could work on different aspects before the final deadline. The result was an unanimously accepted new name, logo, and identity that positioned the organization for growth. Deborah's success in anticipating potential problems took the organization into a new era.

To anticipate potential problems, learn to identify where you might be contributing to them. Build your emotional intelligence skills, and take nothing personally. Then make agreements with your team by assessing trust, listening actively, and doing a premortem. Set benchmarks to check in with the team so you can catch problems early. By being aware of potential problems, you stop conflict before it starts.

Mindset Shifts

---

1. Look to your body regularly to identify your emotions.
2. Don't take anything personally. It's not about you—even if someone says something directly hurtful to you.
3. Watch for evidence of trust, or a lack of it, among the team.
4. Calm your mind so you can listen actively rather than waiting to speak.
5. Believe that people can work around their differences.

New Habits

---

1. Practice emotional intelligence skills. Take steps to become proficient at self-awareness, self-management, social awareness, and relationship management.
2. Look to your body regularly to identify your emotions.
3. Practice identifying your triggers and reactions. Can you catch them earlier each time?
4. Listen actively. Learn to repeat back phrases to be sure you have captured the correct meaning.
5. Do a premortem before every new project or initiative.

3

SET CLEAR EXPECTATIONS

One of my favorite leadership teachers, John C. Maxwell, says, "Disappointment is the gap that exists between expectation and reality." This gap is also a fundamental source of conflict. If you are frustrated and disappointed with results, it's probably because your team doesn't understand what you expect. Setting clear expectations for yourself and your team eases disappointment and defuses conflict. No one is effective without metrics to measure their progress. Conversely, when people know what's expected, they generally rise to the occasion.

As a consultant, I've witnessed many leaders struggle to set clear expectations. Whether they are unsure about roles or don't know how to communicate them, they fail to delineate responsibilities, which leads to confusion and conflict. I have witnessed this frustrating scenario more times than I can count: A leader sets out an exciting plan, paints a strategic vision, gets everyone motivated to begin, even establishes agreements, and then fails to assign tasks to anyone. The team gets excited, but no one does anything, because they don't know what to do. A week goes by, and then a month, and no progress happens. Fast forward to the next team meeting. The leader wants a progress report, and none is forthcoming. The leader gets angry, blames team members for dropping the ball, and creates conflict. The root of the problem wasn't the team members. It was the leader's failure to set clear expectations.

Women struggle with setting expectations more than men. Historically, women played supporting roles in organizations, so only recently have they held leadership positions that required setting expectations. To make the transition from supporter to leader, many women adopted egalitarian models of leadership, which put everyone on an equal level. If you've ever had someone mistake you for a secretary rather than the boss, you know what I mean. Although great for team morale, egalitarian models are terrible for setting expectations. They don't clarify expectations based on varying scopes of responsibilities. Learning to set clear expectations allows women to exert authority without sounding like a bitch.

Your Zone of Genius

Before effectively setting expectations for your team, set realistic expectations for yourself. The key word is *realistic*. Perfectionism runs rampant in female leaders. You don't need to be Wonder Woman to be effective. When you outline impossible goals for yourself, you set yourself up for failure. If you treat yourself that way, you are likely demanding impractical goals from your team too. Unrealistic expectations lead to failure and disappointment, which give way to blame, which devolves into conflict.

To set effective expectations for yourself, identify your strengths. It's a common misconception that success entails overcoming your weaknesses: spending time and energy doing something you don't like isn't as effective as shining at what you love. Well-meaning authority figures may have urged you to focus on improving weak areas because they believed that was the key to success. Unfortunately, it probably taught you to discount your strengths and obsess over your weaknesses, which is ineffective and counterproductive.

Instead, commit to work in your *Zone of Genius*—a term coined by author Gay Hendricks. In his book

The Big Leap, he outlines four zones of activity. He starts with the Zone of Incompetence, which is self-explanatory. Never waste your time on things in your Zone of Incompetence. (For me, it's anything to do with building or managing a web page.) Next is the Zone of Competence. Here you achieve goals and complete tasks, but you're inefficient and miserable. It's best to delegate tasks in these zones.

The third zone, the Zone of Excellence, is the trickiest and most dangerous one. Here you like what you do, you do it well, and you're well-compensated for it. What's the problem? Your Zone of Excellence isn't fulfilling. The tasks drain your energy. As time goes by, it's harder to get motivated. You feel chronic dissatisfaction. Your ability to navigate conflict diminishes as dissatisfaction breeds resentment, frustration, and impatience, which leak out to your team members.

The sweet spot is the Zone of Genius. Here you are in the flow. Everything comes easily. You love what you do and hand over everything else, so work feels fulfilling and enlivening. You shine at your strengths and perform at the highest level. When you live in your Zone of Genius, you rarely instigate conflict within your team. You surround yourself with team members who also work in their Zones of Genius, complementing each other's strengths and operating like a well-oiled machine.

Why doesn't everyone work their Zone of Genius? Simple. You've been taught not to. It's axiomatic that work is supposed to be hard, and if you enjoy it, you're doing something wrong. Many of my female clients admit to feeling guilty about working only in their Zones of Genius. Reframe any idea you have on that score by heeding the words of author Marianne Williamson:

> Our deepest fear is not that we are inadequate. Our deepest fear is that we are powerful beyond measure. It is our light, not our darkness that most frightens us. We ask ourselves, "Who am I to be brilliant, gorgeous, talented, fabulous?" Actually, who are you *not* to be? You are a child of God. Your playing small does not serve the world. There's nothing enlightened about shrinking so that other people won't feel insecure around you.

Once you regularly operate in your Zone of Genius, your limitations become obvious. These are your Zones of Incompetence and Competence. Stay away from them! If you are brilliant at writing but struggle with numbers, don't do bookkeeping. Conversely, if numbers make sense but the thought of speaking in front of a crowd terrifies you, stay behind the scenes, in the accounting department. You have areas where you shine and areas where you struggle. You gain nothing by being critical of your limitations. Everyone has them. Know them, acknowledge them, and look for others who love to do those things.

If you find yourself operating from your Zone of Incompetence or Zone of Competence, be aware that the opportunity for conflict increases. The Twelve-Step tradition of Alcoholics Anonymous uses the acronym HALT to address when someone is on edge. The letters stand for *hungry, angry, lonely*, and *tired*. In these states, humans are more likely to revert to addictions, get triggered, and lose self-control. Working in your limitations puts you in these states, making you more likely to instigate conflict.

Once you've identified your various zones, set firm boundaries around them. Female leaders notoriously struggle to say no. It's probably your willingness to say yes that made you successful in the early part of your career. Although it got you to where you are now, it hinders you from mastering conflict in a position of authority. It seems counterintuitive, but the inability to say no breeds anger and resentment. Without setting firm boundaries, lines of responsibility become blurred, and expectations begin to crumble, inviting misunderstanding. Saying no is more important for effective leadership than saying yes. Remember, *no* is a complete sentence.

Communicate Transparently

After setting clear expectations for yourself, set them for your team. Expectations, however, are only as effective as your communication of them. It's easy to fall into the trap of lazy communication. When you are busy or distracted, it's common to speak in shorthand and ignore how your message is heard, like the hypothetical manager at the beginning of the chapter. Sloppy communication breeds conflict.

To communicate transparently, anticipate what people on your team *hears* rather than what you *say*. Other people don't live inside your head. They haven't had the benefit of following your line of reasoning, knowing your experience, or working toward your desired outcome. Since you see a bigger picture, you must explain unknown variables to the team. You can't afford to assume they understand situations in the way you do. Address all the information the listener needs, even if it feels repetitive to you. Put yourself in their shoes—or, more appropriately, listen through their ears.

Transparent communication operates both ways. Encourage team members to communicate transparently with each other and with you. Establish a high level of clarity as part of your expectations for workplace culture. Unless you work at a top-secret agency, the "need to know" mentality is detrimental to clear expectations.

One caution about transparent communication: it doesn't translate to personnel matters. If a team member drops the ball or has been reprimanded, you can talk about the outcome and the way forward, but not the incident itself. People will want to know all the juicy details, but you can't cross the confidentiality line to indulge in gossip. If someone accuses you of not being transparent, remember that transparency applies to processes and objectives, *not* personnel issues.

Vision

Setting expectations always starts with the organization's vision. If your organization doesn't have a vision statement, create one. Take plenty of time with this, and invite all key stakeholders to participate. There are a variety of resources about writing a powerful vision statement. Find one that works for you. The important thing is that the vision describes why you do what you do. It should excite team members and keep them engaged. If someone isn't aligned with the vision, every single interaction—even the most mundane—is rife with conflict.

A compelling vision keeps everyone moving in the same direction when other systems break down.

As a team works together, it goes through various stages of compatibility. In the first stage, each person looks to the leader for answers. No one feels empowered to think for themselves, so they put their heads down and do what they're told. The problem is you must continually tell them what to do, spending too much time managing day-to-day operations and not enough time actually leading.

To set expectations in this stage, restate the vision. In the absence of a vision, conflict arises. Your team members start to believe their individual ideas are the best, and you'll struggle to reel them back in. Joe from accounting may believe he knows how to run the project, but it differs dramatically from Jane in marketing's idea. You want them to be empowered, but it has to be in service to a unifying vision, not each person's conflicting viewpoint. Communicating a compelling vision that engages everyone gives the whole team ownership of the process.

Next, find the balance between managing tasks and staying out of the weeds. If you live by the mantra that it's easier to do it yourself than to delegate it, beware! Conflict arises when a leader tries to do the work of her subordinates—aka micromanaging. Avoid the urge to micromanage by having detailed job descriptions that outline roles and responsibilities for every position, including yours. If you don't have job descriptions, write them. Include clear lines of reporting and any team affiliations, so everyone understands what their job is and whom they report to. Review job descriptions regularly with team members. Don't just leave them in a file! Quarterly communication about roles and responsibilities works wonders for understanding what's expected.

The Art of Assigning

Once you have the organization's vision and job descriptions, it is time to assign the workload. It sounds like a simple task, but assigning a workload is an art form, much like building a machine. Each part is independent, but they must all work together to achieve the goal. The blueprint is the organizational chart.

The organizational chart doesn't have to be a hierarchical structure with little boxes. I worked for a nonprofit that didn't like hierarchical models. We created a series of concentric circles to show each position's part in the synergistic whole. Every circle encompassed different scopes of responsibility and delineated differences between job categories. Regardless of the format, your org chart should tell who does what at a quick glance. This sounds basic, but the vast majority of companies I worked with have had cluttered and confusing org charts.

When assigning the workload, be transparent about objectives. The greater your team's understanding of the big picture, the more able they will be to fulfill their specific responsibilities. The more detail you give the team about the overall goal, their role in it, and everyone else's part too, the less time you'll waste with conflict-inducing questions and suspicions.

I didn't always appreciate the importance of transparency when assigning tasks. I thought my team should trust me to know what's going on. Why did I need to tell them everything? There were things *they* were responsible for and things *I* was responsible for, and they didn't need to know my business. I started my share of conflict when team members suggested that they couldn't do their work because they needed more information. I felt I had given them everything they needed, and they were being nosy or mistrustful.

Then I remembered one of Stephen Covey's habits for highly successful people—begin with the end in mind. *I* had the end in mind, so I could easily see how things should go, but my team members didn't. How could they possibly know what was expected of them, no matter how many times I explained it? Team members need to see where their project fits into the bigger picture, how they are supposed to work with other departments, and how much latitude they have for their own creativity. Once I mastered transparently assigning tasks, everything became more efficient. I now appreciate the need to overcommunicate objectives when assigning a workload.

A necessary component to assigning tasks is giving directions. Give directions specifically enough to leave no room for misunderstanding, but generally enough to allow team members to do things their way. *Over*explain and qualify as necessary. Don't be obscure. Don't assume they'll understand. I frequently use the phrase, "Let me be crystal clear on this." Focus on objectives, and allow them to develop methods.

A straightforward guide to assigning tasks is the list of question words—who, what, when, where, and why. Begin with *who*. Who exactly is responsible for the project? Explain lines of responsibility and reporting. If two teams are working together on a project, be sure that all team members understand their responsibility. Did you ever get stuck doing a group project in school? Everyone thought that everyone else was going to finish it, right? Remember the rude awakening the week (or day) before the deadline, when you all realized that nobody had done anything? There was always that one person who got away with never doing anything but still shared the grade. If that happens on your teams, conflict will follow. Be sure to set out *who* is responsible, and for what.

Which brings us to *what*. What exactly do you expect as a deliverable? Do you want the whole project completed? Is there a single component that the team must complete first? Do you want one team to vet their contribution through another team, or do you want it to come directly to you? Be clear about the product each person must provide. Explain how the objective fits into the bigger picture, why it is crucial to the overall project, and when it's due.

Speaking of *when*, always provide a time line for each phase of a project. Don't assume that one part of the team will finish before another. If that must be the case, *say so*. If one component depends on another, make sure each team member knows they have a different time line than the rest of the project. Always pad time lines so that a small delay doesn't turn into a big problem. Go over the time lines frequently to ensure the team meets them.

In today's virtual workplace, *where* may not be as critical as it was in the past, but it is still an important factor. If you are putting together a physical product for shipping, consider where each component comes from and how to get them all in the same place. If you are working with intellectual property or a service, consider where the people doing the work are, and if they need to be together in one place. If you need permits, licenses, or other paperwork, know where you get those before you begin.

Through all of the question words, make sure you continually reiterate *why*, which is the vision. Explain *why* you have certain expectations and the importance of each specific piece to the overall success of the whole. Don't let people think their small contribution won't be noticed or doesn't matter. Be so clear about every task's relationship to the vision that even the most menial task takes on a life of its own.

Expectations about workload also include workplace culture. If you expect people to communicate transparently, speak respectfully, or follow a certain code of conduct, make it clear. Don't just say it once or twice. Weave this expectation through every interaction. For example, I expect every team I work with to follow the guidelines of respectful communication as outlined by author John Maxwell in his book, *Ethics 101*.* To that end, I give everyone a hard copy, follow up with an email, and have it laminated and posted around the office. I talk about it in staff meetings and remind people of it when someone starts to disregard the guideline.

_____

* John Maxwell, *Ethics 101: What Every Leader Needs to Know* (New York: Hachette, 2003), 34.

When assigning tasks, include the final project deadline. Providing intermediate time lines is crucial to assigning "when," but be sure everyone knows the deadline for the whole thing. You may be the type of person who immediately gets started on any task and keeps pushing through until it's completed. If so, congratulations! You are a rare breed! More likely, you're like me. I start well, but if I don't know when something is due, time-sensitive things take precedence. Pretty soon, a day, a week, a month, or a quarter has gone by since I last worked on a project, and I have lost both my enthusiasm and momentum. I can let a project linger in limbo forever if I don't have a deadline.

The only way to meet deadlines is to set them! To set a realistic deadline, figure out the drop-dead date for completion. Then, make a "false" deadline one month before that. This becomes the date you give to everyone on your team. I call it the "optimistic" deadline. From this deadline, work backward. Factor in time for approvals, drafts, permits, or whatever is necessary to move to the next step.

Summarize

Assigning tasks takes a lot of repetition. Marketing professionals understand that a person needs to hear something three to five times to remember it. A study done by Microsoft found that it took people between six and twenty repetitions, so the company implemented the Rule of Seven as their policy for repeating important information. Just because you mentioned something in a staff meeting doesn't mean everyone remembers it. Taking time up front to drive the message home saves you time down the road.

A great tool for repetition is to summarize. At the end of every meeting, summarize what you've talked about, and ask everyone to state their responsibilities. People not only need to *hear* information multiple times to comprehend it; they also need to integrate it. When you put the responsibility on them to repeat it back, team members assimilate the information better. I recently accompanied a friend for an outpatient procedure. As the hospital staff prepped her for surgery, both the nurse and the surgeon asked my friend to tell them, in her own words, the procedure they were about to perform. I thought this was a brilliant example of summarizing. By asking people to repeat the information back in their own words, you can be sure they have heard and integrated it.

A colleague of mine used to call it "going around the horn" at the end of the meeting. Once he assigned, discussed, and reviewed tasks, he had every team member summarize what task they were working on and when it was due. Then, if there was a misunderstanding or anything was left out, they caught and corrected it right then and there.

After everyone has reviewed assignments, take the opportunity to reiterate expectations, time lines, and deadlines. It may feel redundant, but repetition decreases conflict. Each time you review tasks, team members gain a deeper understanding of roles, responsibilities, and expectations. Summarizing also sparks conversation about progress on projects as team members accomplish components of them. It feels like you're wasting time at first, but I promise, it saves time in the end.

It is also important to meet in groups rather than one-on-one. Many leaders pride themselves on meeting with each of their direct reports every week, but I discourage it. When you meet with team members one-on-one, you miss the opportunity for group collaboration, discussion, brainstorming, and support. It builds organizational silos and keeps managers from building trust with their peers.

A much better strategy is to meet in peer groups. In Patrick Lencioni's book *Five Dysfunctions of a Team*, he suggests having your "first team," which are people on the same leadership level. If the director of marketing meets only with the marketing team, the marketing department silos and will not work effectively with other departments. However, if all directors meet regularly, they cross-pollinate ideas and take them to their teams to implement. The marketing, sales, accounting, and research departments work better together. This creates greater team cooperation and clearer expectations at all levels of an organization. When you have this degree of buy-in, conflicts are rare.

Role Model: Susan B. Anthony

Perhaps the most important part of setting expectations is role modeling. As anyone who has raised children knows, it never works to ask people to do as you say, not as you do. In their book *The Leadership Challenge*, Jim Kouzes and Barry Posner explain that leaders who set an example through their own behavior and attitude build greater commitment to the organization. They also found that daily acts of living the vision and following the expectations set for the entire team created exponential progress and sparked momentum.

To bring this full circle, setting expectations must both begin and end with you. Once you've identified your Zone of Genius and committed to living from it, you must encourage your team members to do the same. Most importantly, model the behavior continually so your team fully understands expectations.

An outstanding illustration of setting expectations was Susan B. Anthony, the nineteenth-century American social reformer and women's suffrage advocate. Anthony was born in 1820 into a family committed to social equality. Her parents and siblings were ardent abolitionists and temperance advocates. At age twenty-six, Anthony became the headmistress of the female department of an educational academy in Canajoharie, New York. This was her first experience with unequal treatment of women, and she bristled at receiving less pay than men in her field for the same job.

Anthony quickly identified her Zone of Genius. Although she worked as a teacher and also ran her family farm, she excelled at organizing, speaking, and motivating others. She embarked on her career of social reform as a way to take advantage of her gifts and contribute to causes she believed in. Her experience at the Canajoharie Academy helped her identify her limitations and prompted her to set firm boundaries. She would not work for less than she was worth, and continually advocated equal pay for women. She also left her family farm to become a speaker, and for the rest of her life earned her living doing what she loved.

In 1851, Anthony met another social reformer, Elizabeth Cady Stanton, and the two formed a partnership that benefited both greatly. Anthony found that Stanton's skills complemented her own, and they made an effective team, allowing both to operate in their Zones of Genius. Whereas Anthony loved to speak and motivate, Stanton was more introverted and preferred writing and exploring intellectual ideas. Stanton also had seven children, so she could not travel the way Anthony, who was single, could. Stanton wrote treatises about equality, and Anthony embraced the ideas and took them on the road. Stanton's husband, Henry Brewster Stanton, described how the pair worked: "Susan stirred the pudding, Elizabeth stirred up Susan, and Susan stirred up the world."

Because of the clarity of expectations she set for herself, Anthony used her organizing skills to create multiple social reform organizations. Between 1837 and 1868, she was foundationally involved in organizations to promote temperance, abolish slavery, and provide equal rights for women. In 1868, when the Fifteenth Amendment to the Constitution was proposed, providing voting rights to black men but omitting women, both black and white, Anthony began organizing the movement that become her longest-lasting legacy.

Anthony gathered her team, including Stanton and other women's rights activists, to form the American Equal Rights Association (AERA). Anthony and Stanton began publishing a weekly newspaper called *The Revolution*, in which they outlined the organization's compelling vision: "Men, their rights and nothing more; women, their rights and nothing less." Unfortunately, the AERA split over the issue of the Fifteenth Amendment.

Anthony, ever the organizer, was undaunted. She immediately created the National Women's Suffrage Association, and in this context, her skills for setting clear expectations are obvious. The vision of the organization was the passage of a constitutional amendment allowing women to vote. In addition to setting the vision, she effortlessly assigned tasks to the members, from fundraising to advocacy work to lobbying. Contemporary accounts recall that Anthony's outstanding communication skills helped her clearly delineate who, what, when, where, and why activities took place. Anthony trained younger activists, who became known as her "nieces," to assume leadership roles so that the movement would have continuity. After a few missteps with failed alliances with other organizations, Anthony articulated clear expectations among her team by speaking to each member and having them summarize their responsibilities.

Anthony certainly acted as a role model for the equal rights of women in social and political culture.

In post–Civil War America, she showed that a single woman, then called by the unflattering name "spinster," could emerge on the national scene as a powerful leader. By the 1880s, she was one of the senior political figures in the United States of either gender. She lived her values, launching legal challenges to laws that prohibited women from voting. The basis for these challenges was language in the Fourteenth Amendment that said, "No State shall make or enforce any law which shall abridge the privileges or immunities of citizens of the United States." When Anthony was arrested for voting illegally in 1872, her trial became a cause célèbre. Although she was found guilty, the judge waived the fine.

Although the Nineteenth Amendment to the Constitution, enacting women's suffrage, did not pass until August 18, 1920—fourteen years after Anthony's death—the expectations she set and the team she built made it possible. The National Women's Suffrage Association peacefully protested, but never instigated or advocated conflict. They also had minimal conflict within their organization, considering the magnitude of the work they did. Anthony was clear about the expectations she had for herself, and role-modeled the vision she set.

Leadership through a Merger

You don't have to be an avid reformer to successfully set clear expectations. One of my clients, Amanda, learned to set clear expectations while leading her company through a merger.

She had limited time to do it. Amanda recognized that the two organizations had similar visions but very different systems, policies, and procedures. Like Susan B. Anthony incorporating diverse opinions, Amanda had to use different methods to bring everyone together.

Amanda set realistic expectations for herself. She knew her Zone of Genius, which was relationship building. She avoided her limitations and established clear boundaries. She refused to do detail work, which fell into her Zone of Incompetence. She also avoided polarized thinking. She set boundaries around anyone trying to force her to choose sides in the process.

When she started meeting with the merger teams, Amanda communicated transparently. She assigned tasks, addressing the who, what, when, where, and particularly the why. She summarized assignments at every meeting and asked team members to repeat them back. She tied every decision back to the vision.

Once Amanda set expectations, she built teams to implement aspects of the merger. Each team had an objective punctuated by time lines. Every department had to evaluate its business practices, come up with a best-practices list, and create action steps to revise two sets of practices into one. Amanda met regularly with the various teams, reiterating expectations and maintaining time lines.

Amanda was also a role model. Whenever anything happened to stall the process, she looked at it as an opportunity to find a better solution. She reconvened everyone, went through roles, responsibilities, and objectives, and asked for feedback. She never allowed herself to get frustrated or discouraged. Consequently, she was able to lead these two somewhat antagonistic organizations through a merger in less than a year, with minimal conflict.

Amanda knew her expectations were successful when at one point a member of one of the organizations started to create conflict about the education and training department. This member questioned the new process and demanded reverting to the way one of the previous organizations had done it. To Amanda's delight, her team *jointly* addressed the issue, outlined the vision, explained the objectives, set a clear boundary, and managed the conflict before it escalated.

Setting clear expectations is the cornerstone of mastering conflict. As wonderful as it would be to believe that all conflict starts outside of yourself, it is imperative to remember that your expectations for yourself are the primary indicator of how smoothly conflict gets handled. When you identify your Zone of Genius, stay away from your limitations, and learn to say no, you avoid being the source of conflict on your team.

The key to setting expectations is transparent communication. If your team doesn't know what you mean, they certainly can't implement it. Assigning a workload, summarizing responsibilities, and creating time lines all create a baseline of expectations without the confusion that frequently leads to conflict.

Finally, live the expectations you set. Don't be a hypocrite and tell the team one thing while you do another. Role-model the work ethic and culture you desire, even as you are clear about the separation of roles and responsibilities. It is amazing how much this first step does to help you master conflict.

Mindset Shifts

1. Set realistic expectations for yourself.
2. Identify your Zone of Genius. What do you love to do? What comes easily for you? If you are struggling with this, take an online test or see a coach to determine your unique gifts.
3. Think in terms of the question words: *who? what? where? when? why?* Practice thinking through the answers to all of them.
4. Learn to release guilt. It's not your responsibility to make anybody happy but yourself
5. Take time to think. Get clear about objectives before taking action.

New Habits

1. Practice self-care. Give yourself a break every day.
2. Listen to your team's perspective and adapt your communication strategy accordingly.
3. Practice saying no to things. If you don't feel a full-body yes when you are asked to do something, set a clear boundary.
4. Be transparent. Unless something involves a personnel matter, ask yourself if you can be even more transparent with your team.
5. Live within the expectations you set for everyone else.

4

HOLD PEOPLE ACCOUNTABLE

Now that you've set expectations, it is also your responsibility to ensure everyone lives up to them. Wouldn't life be grand if every team member did exactly what they were supposed to?

Unfortunately, that is seldom the case. Establishing agreements and setting expectations are important steps, but you must enforce them by holding individuals accountable.

What does it mean to hold someone accountable? Accountability is frequently confused with blame. Identifying and correcting what went wrong is part of the meaning of accountability, but it has a broader definition. Holding people accountable means ensuring team members keep their agreements. It's a difficult thing to do, because it takes courage to tell someone they haven't done a good job, failed in some way, disappointed you, or let the team down. It feels as if you're creating conflict. Yet, as uncomfortable as many people find it, holding people accountable is critical for reducing opportunities for conflict.

Holding people accountable requires all of your emotional intelligence skills. It's tempting to blame someone, especially if you're convinced that he or she acted willfully, but exercise self-management. Everyone makes mistakes. Address and correct the mistake kindly, without blaming. Let go of any people-pleasing tendencies, and remember that requiring team members to keep their agreements doesn't create conflict. In the long run, pointing out broken agreements and asking for correction reduces conflict, keeping you from having to be a bitch.

Identify Personal Missteps

Before you hold anyone else accountable, start with yourself. Have you kept your agreements? Are you meeting expectations? Ask your team for feedback, and be open to hearing what they say. It's intimidating to open yourself up to potential criticism, but you can't know how you're doing if you don't hear from the people you're doing it with. Get into a regular habit of asking your team members about your agreements and expectations. You can also do a leadership assessment, using a 360 tool or team surveys to get honest responses. (A 360 tool is an evaluation system whereby employees receive confidential, anonymous feedback from coworkers.)

Take the feedback for what it's worth. It's a great opportunity to practice not taking anything personally. Don't let it destroy your confidence, but do let it inform how you interact with the team. Look for patterns in your behavior and allow them to raise your self-awareness. If you have set expectations for a supportive culture, you shouldn't have to worry about mean-spirited or hurtful comments. Not every observation will be accurate. Your team isn't privy to everything you do, so their perception is necessarily skewed. But use their observations to hold yourself accountable.

If you have broken an agreement, missed a deadline, or fostered some misunderstanding, apologize. Don't say you're sorry for every little thing, but take responsibility when necessary. Many leaders feel it's inappropriate to apologize to their team because it weakens the chain of command. This detrimental and hypocritical mindset signals to the team that there is a different set of rules for you than for them. If you want to be credible, you must also be accountable.

As you look for personal missteps, take the opportunity to clarify your objectives. It's easy to start a project with one set of objectives, then shift your priorities as you get more information. Objectives morph over time. It becomes an accountability issue, however, if you have revised objectives in your own mind but have never told your team about them. The changes can affect your team members' roles and consequently confuse agreements and expectations. Be sure you are still operating from the same objectives you were in the beginning. If you perceive that a team member has broken an agreement when in reality you changed the rules, the accountability resides with you.

Courageous Conversations

Courageous conversations are exactly what they sound like—conversations that demand courage. Our culture goes out of its way to avoid courageous conversations. The classic example is the pleasantries exchanged with just about everyone: "How are you?" No one really wants an answer to that question. You are expected to say, "Fine." If you stopped on the street and answered the question truthfully, people would think you were crazy!

Instead of a courageous conversation, many leaders use the "sandwich" method to hold subordinates accountable. The leader focuses on what a team member is doing *right*, subtly slips in a quick phrase about what the person could do better, then ends with what's going *right*. It is called the sandwich method because you begin and end with the good things so the person doesn't feel criticized, demoralized, or demotivated. The idea is reasonable and kind, but the execution rarely works. The meat of the conversation gets lost in between.

I had a boss who tried the sandwich method with me. In college, I worked as a cashier in a clothing store. Apparently I was doing something wrong on the point-of-sale machine. I had been taught to ring up sales incorrectly and didn't realize it. When my boss brought me in to his office to address the issue, he told me how wonderful I was with customers, how much he appreciated my friendly attitude, and how many compliments I got from customers. He then talked about discrepancies in the end-of-day reports and how important it was to be accurate. He asked if I understood. I said yes, because I thought I did. I agreed that it was important to be accurate. He ended the meeting, and I left relatively confused.

Two weeks later, he called me back into the office. He was less friendly this time. He was prepared for a huge conflict. He acted as if I had willfully disobeyed him, or, worse, was stealing. He was ready to take disciplinary action. When I asked him what was wrong, he looked at me as if I was an idiot. He got angry and condescendingly told me what I was doing wrong. That was the first time I realized what he meant. After I explained that I didn't get that message at the first meeting, things calmed down, and we were ultimately able to laugh about it. But I always remembered how much easier it would have been if he hadn't beaten around the bush the first time.

Courageous conversations avoid the problems of the sandwich method. Most people assume that courageous conversations are destructive when actually they defuse conflict. They require that each party feels safe to share honestly. Most people don't have the emotional intelligence to be vulnerable for a courageous conversation. Without bringing hidden emotions to the surface, however, colleagues allow small slights and minor incidents to fester and become sources of conflict. When the small stuff is discussed openly, each person can take responsibility before the potential problem becomes a big deal.

Foundational to courageous conversations is a courageous culture, where difficult conversations are the norm rather than an exception. Courageous culture is built on absolute candor and allows team members to speak up when they feel something's wrong. It's ironic that most people *don't* say what they mean, thinking it will avoid conflict, when actually it leads to hidden agendas, anger, and resentment that are the sources of conflict. I'm not suggesting that you be in everyone's face. Don't be sarcastic or snide. Don't hint at what you mean or imply things you hope the other person will understand. Don't be unpleasant or bring up difficult topics at inappropriate times.

Having a courageous culture means being direct, clear, and vulnerable. Take time to say what's wrong, and talk about underlying issues. Trust team members to be supportive.

These conversations are important at work, but they are useful in all areas of life. If you avoid telling a loved one that something hurt your feelings because you don't want to appear vulnerable or complaining, you are missing an opportunity to deepen your relationship and have your needs met. If you don't talk about your achievements to friends because you don't want to brag, you're missing an opportunity to get support. Communicating feelings and perceptions is a critical skill.

There are three necessary components to a courageous conversation: have empathy, ask questions, and tell the truth.

Have Empathy

Courageous conversations require empathy. Most people don't understand empathy. It is frequently confused with sympathy, but the two are practically opposites. Sympathy means having compassion for someone who's experiencing misfortune. It has the connotation of pity; for that reason, most people don't want sympathy. In other cases, a person goes to the other extreme and seeks sympathy to get attention. They want to be victims. In any case, people who are either looking for or avoiding sympathy are not operating in the present moment. They are reacting from a past trigger, which isn't conducive to a courageous conversation.

Unlike sympathy, empathy means putting yourself in the other person's position and understanding their experience. Empathy requires being radically present with the other person. Whereas sympathy puts someone in the role of victim, empathy empowers the other person by offering understanding and support. When you empathize, you are viewing the other person's experience from his or her perspective, thereby validating it.

This empowering aspect of empathy prevents conflict in a courageous conversation. If someone is invested in being a victim, you'll have trouble holding that person accountable, no matter how much evidence you have of a broken agreement. But if you fully understand what that person is feeling, you can help them shift from feeling like a victim to being empowered. Once this shift happens, there's little likelihood things will devolve into conflict.

Ask Questions

When you begin a courageous conversation, start with questions. If there's a broken agreement, don't immediately assume that someone did something wrong. Find out what happened, and hear all perspectives. Get in the right frame of mind so you aren't nervous about a possible confrontation, leading you to stumble through it. If you're trying to get it over quickly, your questions will come out too aggressively, and it will sound as if you're interrogating a suspect. Your discomfort will be misconstrued, making the other person defensive and closing off all possibility of a true, open conversation.

Before starting the conversation, think of several questions to focus your thinking and clarify assumptions. For example, if you're addressing someone for failing to finish a project on time, don't jump to the conclusion that the person has faulty time management skills or didn't take the project seriously. Ask questions like, "What was your understanding of the requirements for the project?" Or "Did you know that several other departments were involved in the time line?" Be careful that the questions aren't accusatory or provocative. Ask simply for information and clarification. Keep your tone light and inquisitive. Listen carefully. You will learn information that changes how you approach accountability.

A great question is "How would you handle things if you were in my position?" It helps break down oppositional energy and urges the other person think beyond their own situation. It also encourages them to take the bigger picture into account. Most importantly, it starts a dialogue that can lead to a courageous conversation.

Tell the Truth

Once you've asked questions, start the accountability conversation by telling the truth. State the facts clearly, and keep any judgment out of it. Don't make the person wrong for making a mistake. If someone was supposed to do something and didn't, state what was supposed to happen, and ask why it didn't. If something happened that wasn't supposed to, state the facts and ask why it happened.

Evaluating behavior is different from passing judgment. Don't make the person feel bad, shame them, or criticize them. You've had bad days and done stupid things. Think of the line from the 1960s TV show *Dragnet*: "Just the facts, ma'am." When people feel blamed, they become defensive, which starts a vicious cycle of recrimination and justification. Avoid this cycle by just telling the truth.

When telling the truth, practice self-management so you detach any superfluous emotions from the conversation. If you have any anger at the person you're holding accountable, process it before you have a conversation with them. Similarly, if you feel sad or guilty about something in the situation, straighten out your own emotions so that you can tell the truth without being influences by your personal reactions.

It sounds so straightforward, doesn't it? Unfortunately, humans are trained to believe that someone must be right and someone else must be wrong. This cultural paradigm keeps people from admitting mistakes and taking responsibility. Instead of telling the truth, they twist it to support their case. It doesn't have to work that way. When you state the facts rather than drawing battle lines, it defuses conflict while addressing what needs to change. There is no need for antagonism. Just clearly and directly address what happened, what didn't, and ask plenty of questions.

Courageous conversations sometimes bring up unresolved issues in both you and the other person, especially around authority figures. It is not reasonable to assume that employees will leave their personal issues at home. Leaders have to expect that team members may have unhealed authority issues that are played out at work. If an otherwise good staff person reacts negatively to a courageous conversation, go back and restate agreements and expectations. By stating the facts, you remind the person you're talking about professional behavior, not personal failings.

Becoming proficient at courageous conversations takes both courage and practice. Exhibiting empathy, asking questions, and telling the truth create a solid foundation for a team with a courageous culture. When team members aren't afraid to talk about what's going on below the surface, there are fewer opportunities for conflict.

Coach Rather than Correct

Courageous conversations are most successful when you approach them as coaching rather than correcting. More than ever, leaders must be coaches and mentors rather than bosses. The coaching aspects of your role allow you to help team members succeed by motivating, inspiring, and focusing them. Only address obstacles that keep the team from the goal.

You laid the groundwork for coaching when you established agreements and set expectations. From this foundation, feedback is fact-based and easy to deliver. Is the person delivering on her commitments? Is she working well with other stakeholders? If she needs to increase output, is she on track? The feedback can also go both ways: should you be doing anything to be more supportive? Give feedback weekly, and remember it's more important to be helpful than nice. That doesn't mean you can be a bitch, but it does mean you must tell the truth.

If expectations haven't been met, look for patterns. From there, create a coaching framework to adjust the negative patterns and replace them with productive habits. Being outcome-driven requires staying focused on the ultimate success of the project rather than placing blame. Most people want to do a good job. I don't assume that people are trying to goof off, ignore their responsibilities, or be indifferent. When people have quality leadership, they excel and become part of a winning team. But they have to be coached with honest feedback and clear accountability. If you want someone to do something differently, know exactly what you want and state it clearly.

Like any good coach, detach your personal feelings about any given team member. Perhaps you are working with someone who annoys you. Maybe this person is brash and loud, or perhaps meek and unassuming. If this trait rubs you the wrong way, you might be prone to find fault with them even if they've done nothing wrong. Just because you don't like the *way* someone does something doesn't make it wrong, so long as they accomplish the task and play within the team agreements. However, if they are doing something that violates team agreements, clarify exactly what that is. When you address it, state without reservation or confusion what the person needs to correct. Keep your personal opinion to yourself.

Similarly, detach from personal feelings about team members you like. If you have a great relationship with someone, joke around, and look forward to catching up every morning, you must be willing to hold this person accountable too. It may be more pleasant to coach this person, but you have to remain impartial. The rules apply equally to everyone. Failure to be neutral leads to accusations of favoritism, destroys morale, and creates conflict.

One way to avoid sounding argumentative when giving feedback is to use the word *and* instead of *but*. *But* is a signal you are about to contradict what the other person said. By using *and,* you recognize that their version of the story and your version of the story coexist. For example, if you are having a courageous conversation with an employee (let's call her Jill) who is constantly late for work, it might sound like this:

YOU: You have been late for work for three of the past ten days. That's a 30 percent late ratio, and that's unacceptable. (State the facts.)

JILL: I know, and I'm really sorry, but I'm having car trouble, and I can't afford to get it fixed.

YOU: That's a tough break. I'm sorry to hear that. (Empathy.) *And* you have a responsibility to your team to be here on time.

You aren't negating the seriousness of her situation. You're using empathy to show you understand. However, you are continuing to state that the other person has responsibilities to meet. Using *and* instead of *but* opens the door for a conversation that allows the two of you to fulfill or renegotiate the agreement. You are creating a third way that joins "your" way and "her" way for mutual benefit. Renegotiating might sound like this:

YOU: How long do you think your car will be a problem?

JILL: It's two weeks until I can get the funds to fix it, and another week in the shop.

YOU: Do you need to renegotiate agreements?

JILL: That would help! Can I work remotely two days per week for the next three weeks?

YOU: It works for me, *and* we need to check with the rest of the team.

Saying *and* instead of *but* keeps the other person from getting defensive. Defensiveness rarely leads to a supportive, productive conversation. By saying *and*, you are acknowledging the reality of their experience while emphasizing their need to keep their agreements.

Once you've coached a team member to a solution, follow through on your action plans. Don't give people corrective feedback and then never talk about it again. Once you have held someone accountable, you've entered a coaching relationship with them, so don't leave them hanging. Have regular meetings to discuss progress. For example, check back in with Jill to see how her car's doing and if she's able to come back to the office in the agreed-upon time frame.

The best way to become an expert at accountability and coaching is practice. Practice in the mirror, or better yet, have a friend, partner, or spouse role-play with you. The more courageous conversations you have, the easier it is to think on your feet. If you're role playing with someone else, give them the freedom to make it hard on you! You want to be able to address anything that comes up in an actual meeting. If you can practice without getting flustered, you will do much better when the time actually comes. Holding people accountable is never easy, but it doesn't have to be hard.

Accountability and the Queen

One of the greatest historical examples of holding people accountable was a figure from recent history, Queen Elizabeth II of the United Kingdom. Elizabeth was never meant to be queen. Her date with destiny started in 1936, when her uncle, King Edward VIII, abdicated the throne to marry an American divorcée, Wallis Simpson. This propelled Elizabeth's father onto the throne as King George VI, and the young Princess Elizabeth into position as his heir. King George died in 1952, thrusting Elizabeth onto the throne at the age of twenty-five. As a young wife and mother, Queen Elizabeth wasn't what her subjects expected. She learned early in her reign that to be taken seriously, she had to hold people accountable.

There are hundreds of examples of the queen holding people accountable to maintain the monarchy and avoid conflict throughout her long reign. Thanks to the Netflix program *The Crown*, a new generation is familiar with Elizabeth's magnificent ability to hold herself accountable and identify her own missteps. She publicly committed herself to a life of service and had the humility to admit when she fell short. The most memorable instance of the queen admitting her missteps occurred with her handling of the divorce of her son, Prince Charles, from Princess Diana and Diana's subsequent sudden death. The queen realized she was out of touch with public sentiment, admitted it, and went on live television to correct it.

Over the decades, Queen Elizabeth repeatedly had to have courageous conversations with others, ranging from her closest advisors to luminaries such as Winston Churchill, John F. Kennedy, and her sister, Princess Margaret. She gained an impeccable reputation for her empathy, her ability to ask questions, and her candor. She did not allow the standards of behavior to weaken, but maintained affectionate relationships.

A prime example of the queen's ability to hold someone accountable came in 2022 with the handling of her son, Prince Andrew, and his association with the sex trafficking case against Jeffrey Epstein. Although Prince Andrew denied all wrongdoing, the subsequent trial and scandal threatened to taint the royal family. Rather than drag the family through a prolonged conflict by defending her son, Queen Elizabeth held him accountable to the agreements he made as a working royal. She asked questions, clearly had empathy for her middle son, and told the truth about the situation and the threat it posed to the royal family. Although still a member of the family, she removed him from all of his royal duties and patronages, sending a message that she would not tolerate broken agreements.

Handling Mismanaged Finances

You don't have to be the queen of England to be skilled at holding people accountable. Claire was the CEO of a California-based company that moved its headquarters to a new state to take advantage of lower real estate prices. Shortly after moving, Claire found that the finances were mismanaged. The funds allocated for the move had been previously earmarked for other purposes, leaving the company on the brink of bankruptcy. Claire had been depending on the chief operating officer to manage all operations, including finances, and was shocked by the news.

First, Claire identified her missteps. As CEO, she should have been more aware of the situation. She put too much faith in the COO and hadn't been involved enough. Claire disclosed the situation to the board of directors, took responsibility, and apologized. Despite her apology, the board wanted to know who exactly had made the mistakes that left the organization in this precarious position. Although Claire had an idea who was responsible, she called a meeting of her executive team. She expressed empathy for everyone on the team. Two members, hired after the move, had joined a company that was almost bankrupt. The COO moved with the organization and purchased a house. Each executive team member had legitimate reasons to be afraid for the future. Claire empathized with everyone's situation.

Next, Claire asked questions. She didn't blame anyone or jump to conclusions. She inquired about the finances. She questioned what each executive knew about the move. She asked everyone to remind her of their roles. She questioned why the situation wasn't identified earlier and why she hadn't been informed of progress along the benchmarks that had been set. She carefully listened to the answers.

By the end of the process, Claire realized the COO had made a critical error in budgeting the move. He hadn't allowed enough for expenses and had misappropriated funds to cover the mistake. Claire set the expectation that the move was his project to successfully complete, and he failed. They had agreements about the move that hadn't been kept.

After a couple of weeks investigating what went wrong, asking questions, and determining responsibility for the mistakes, Claire called the COO and told the truth. She didn't blame, offer recriminations, or point fingers. She stated the fact that it was the COO's responsibility to manage the move, and he didn't pay attention to the necessary information. She expressed empathy for the fact that he was trying to move, but plainly stated that she could no longer depend on him for the organization's operations and let him go. She didn't start a fight, accuse, or create conflict. She told the truth and moved on. Meanwhile, she coached the remaining executives on how to handle the ensuing financial fallout.

To hold people accountable, identify any missteps you might have made or agreements you may have broken, have courageous conversations, and coach rather than correct. Build the confidence to ask questions, have empathy, and tell the truth, no matter how difficult. No matter how predisposed you are to avoid interpersonal strife, holding people accountable is one of the most valuable skills for clarifying agreements and expectations. Holding people accountable doesn't create conflict. It avoids it.

Mindset Shifts

1. Take personal inventory of any mistakes you've made or agreements you've broken. Apologize if necessary.
2. Don't be afraid to ask for honest feedback from your team.
3. Continually review your objectives.
4. Look for situations that call for empathy. Let go of judgment and be present with the other person.
5. Understand that you can't hurt other people by telling the truth.

New Habits

1. Practice recognizing the difference between sympathy and empathy.
2. Ask questions.
3. Tell the truth without any superfluous emotions.
4. Disengage personal feeling from professional situations.
5. Catch yourself when you want to say "but" and switch it to "and."

5

OVERCOME RESISTANCE

No matter how proficient you get at holding someone accountable, as soon as you do it, resistance surfaces. It's human nature.

First, resistance may arise in you as you prepare for the conversation. Depending on how comfortable you are with conflict, resistance might include dreading the interaction. Similarly, resistance shows up in your team members when they justify and defend their actions. It's understandable, since most people learn to get defensive or blame someone else if they think they're in trouble. The person you're talking to probably doesn't view it as resistance. They believe they are simply offering a good "reason why." Resistance, however, is frequently the basis for conflict.

Resistance differs from legitimate reasons. Occasionally, there are valid reasons for making a mistake or missing a deadline. Everyone gets sick, family emergencies happen, the power goes off, and you oversleep. Providing a reason for a one-time occurrence doesn't necessarily have a lot of emotional energy behind it. Resistance, however, chronically manifests as excuses and objections, and is almost always a cover-up for one of three behaviors: failing to prioritize an agreement, declining to take expectations seriously, or believing the individual won't be held accountable.

I had a choir teacher once who had two strict rules. The first rule: no chewing gum! Period. He pointed out that you can't sing with gum in your mouth, and of course he was right. That wasn't really what made him unique, though; most teachers had rules against gum. What made him unique was the second rule: if you were caught chewing gum, you couldn't say you were sorry. He didn't want to hear it. He said, "Don't be sorry, be smart." He understood that any excuse a student offered was just a cover for their failure to take his rule seriously.

The punishment for either offense—chewing gum or saying you were sorry for chewing gum—was to be kicked out of two class periods. If you chewed gum and then apologized, you missed four classes. Since the grade was attendance-based, this had severe consequences. The teacher's point was that we were warned. There was absolutely *no* good reason for chewing gum in his class. He told us not to do it; he told us what would happen if we did; we all agreed; end of story. Yet every class period, someone was caught chewing gum, and more often than not, the first word out of her mouth was "sorry." His example has stuck with me as a morality tale about prioritizing agreements and expectations.

One of my personal pet peeves is people who say they've run out of time to get a Christmas gift. Christmas falls on the same day every year. You could buy Christmas gifts for your entire family right now for the rest of their lives, if you could plan that well. (Understandably, there are legitimate reasons not to: their tastes change; you don't know your budget; you could have a falling-out.) Running out of time isn't a reason. It's a lazy way of saying, "This wasn't important enough for me to think about earlier." It is an emotional response rooted in the limbic brain, overriding the rational, behavioral-oriented cerebral cortex.

Fear triggers resistance. Since many people believe they can get away with breaking agreements, the thought of being held accountable triggers a variation of the fight-or-flight response. If you're the leader holding a team member accountable, expect resistance. To overcome it, find the balance between being empathetic and getting results. Start by addressing your own resistance and adjusting your behavior so you don't have to act like a bitch.

Reframe Your Internal Conversation

It's easy to see resistance in someone else, but it's harder to find it in yourself. To identify your resistance, monitor your inner dialogue and reframe that internal conversation. When something goes wrong, do you immediately blame someone? Approaching a conversation with accusatory energy—no matter what you actually say—immediately makes the other person defensive. As soon as the other person feels blamed, excuses fly, and conflict is imminent.

Avoid this dynamic by shifting how you think about the situation. From my experience, courageous conversations start calmly, but after you've said your initial, practiced statement and the other person has offered resistance (defensiveness, excuses, objections), it's easy to lose your composure and meet their energy with similar resistance. Reframing *your* internal conversation is crucial. Do your best to stay out of the limbic brain and in the rational cerebral cortex. Regardless of the resistance you meet, stay focused on your breathing to avoid matching that energy.

Almost every excuse is a variation of "I ran out of time" or "Something else came up." When I was a college professor, I heard all sorts of variations on these themes. I listened to multiple iterations of the "grandparent died" excuse. The death rate among the elderly must have skyrocketed in those years! That excuse is just "something else came up" in dramatic form. Recognizing common themes helps you stay rational and even anticipate the types of excuses you'll get.

Anticipating common excuses gives you practice in establishing the energy you bring to the conversation. Keep from being confrontational by approaching situations with curiosity. Be curious why something happened, or how the person chose to make the decision they did. When you're curious, you release accusations, and the conversation becomes heartfelt and sincere rather than oppositional. When you hold someone accountable, you are not trying to get an admission of guilt. You are trying to get results. Being curious allows for an open dialogue and shifts the dynamic from accusatory to outcome-oriented.

Release any urge to get angry. If someone drops the ball, then gives you an excuse, it's understandable that you'd get mad. As a matter of fact, it's probably typical, but you simply can't afford it. Anger makes mistakes personal when they don't need to be. Getting angry at a team member shuts that person down and keeps her from hearing suggestions. It also causes her to dig into a position and be unwilling to consider a different perspective.

When I started holding people accountable, I met every kind of resistance. At first, excuses annoyed me. The angrier I got, however, the more I contributed to the oppositional energy of the conversation. When I stopped being annoyed, I got better results. Now I find excuses rather creative.

Your anger also hardens the other person's resistance. If you get angry, what might have started as a mild excuse can escalate into an objection to everything you say. The more intense your emotions are, the more intense the reaction is. Newton's third law states that for every action there is an equal and opposite reaction. If you refrain from getting angry, there's no necessity for objections or argument. Using curiosity, steer the conversation into the more productive space of asking what they would do differently.

Resistance Busters

As stated above, people on your team exhibit resistance in three primary ways—excuses, objections, and disengagement. Team members use excuses to get out of an obligation or promise. Objections are a more intense form of resistance, offering argument, disagreement, refusal, or disapproval. Disengagement is the subtlest form, but also the most destructive, because it's hard to catch. Disengagement means the person is going through the motions without contributing.

Try these resistance busters with your team members: One of the most disarming ways to defuse resistance is to welcome it. If you meet resistance with resistance, you get more resistance. Try pushing your hand against a friend's hand. The harder she pushes, the harder you push back. Now stop pushing altogether. All resistance stops. Dropping all resistance and welcoming whatever happens breaks the cycle.

Welcoming resistance means being unfailingly kind while unyieldingly firm. Kindness dissolves resistance. It is strategic, whereas anger is reactionary. Be clear, direct, and firm, but couple those traits with kindness in order to disarm excuses and objections. No matter what reason you have to hold someone accountable, combining kindness with firm insistence makes it difficult to argue about requested corrections.

The key to welcoming resistance with kindness is maintaining control of your emotions and supporting the other person in doing the same. Being firm and direct lets team members know that you are serious about the topic and its consequences. Kindness also lets them know you're open to constructive solutions.

Another effective resistance buster is something I call "playing dumb." Instead of meeting resistance with rational arguments, justifications, or intimidation, playing dumb offers complete nonresistance without triggering dangerous emotions in you or the other person.

I learned how to play dumb over twenty-five years ago, when my daughter was two years old. The approach doesn't come from a leadership manual, but from a book entitled *Parenting with Love and Logic* by Foster Cline and Jim Fay. I used this technique successfully with my daughter when she was a toddler and again when she was a teenager. As helpful as it was for parenting, I have used this strategy most successfully in professional contexts.

The basic premise of playing dumb is to defuse resistance by refusing to participate in it. It takes two people to argue, and if you remove yourself, the other person has nowhere to go. The technique entails finding a phrase and repeating it ad nauseam until the other person runs out of excuses or objections. Once the other person gets exhausted trying to think of a new objection, she generally comes to a solution on her own. Either that, or she will drop the argument altogether and accept the agreement as originally stated.

Here is a real-life example from a situation with my daughter where I played dumb and overcame her resistance. She was fifteen years old and had just recovered from mononucleosis. She wanted to go to an all-night party with her 4-H leadership team. It was chaperoned and programmed, but I didn't want her staying up all night. She needed sleep. She had barely recovered enough to go back to school, and I didn't think her health could take an all-nighter. I told her she couldn't go.

The excuses, objections, and whining started immediately. She said, "But all my friends are going!" I didn't argue with her. This is a crucial point. Don't argue! If you do, you're just offering resistance to the resistance. I agreed with her and repeated my bottom-line phrase: "I'm sure they are going, and you're not." She tried several other attempts, like "I promise I'll get some sleep," and "I will come home and sleep all day the next day," to which I said things like, "I'm sure you will, and you're not going." Finally, she hit below the belt. She said, "You just don't love me!" As easy as it would have been to take that bait, I didn't. I simply replied, "I love you very much, and you're not going." Then she said—and this was the tough one—"I hate you!" To which I replied, again, "That's too bad, because I love you very much, and you're not going."

At no point did I get outwardly mad or frustrated. I never argued with her or contradicted her points. I just kept empathizing with her situation and telling her she wasn't going. Needless to say, she didn't go. About three weeks after the event, when she'd heard all about it from her friends, she said to me, "Mom, I'm glad I didn't go. I wouldn't have gotten any sleep, it didn't sound like that much fun, and everyone else got colds from being there." Score one for playing dumb.

While your team members probably won't say, "I hate you," they can try to manipulate you in other ways. I had a staff member who kept dropping the ball on a marketing campaign. She wanted to go in a different direction, but for many reasons, I disagreed. Because she didn't support the campaign, she procrastinated and made mistakes. She came into my office daily with preemptive excuses about why something wouldn't get done. She always offered her favorite alternative, which we had extensively discussed. I didn't try to make her see my side or prove that I was right. I just kept saying, "I understand you want to do something differently. Thanks for sharing. Now let's get back on track." No matter how many times she came into my office, she got the same answer every time. I didn't mind if she thought I was an idiot. I knew better, and I didn't waste valuable time and energy arguing with someone whose mind I wasn't going to change. She finally implemented the campaign.

To play dumb, you have to be secure in your leadership. Most leaders want everyone to agree with them. Sometimes it's important to have broad buy-in, but it isn't necessary for most operational decisions. Give up caring what others think, and stay focused on the goal. You have the authority to do things your way, so don't waste time managing conflict that won't change the end result. If you don't need the team's agreement, don't argue. Just move on.

Another powerful resistance buster is reengagement. If you continually meet resistance despite trying other methods, it is probably because a team member has lost excitement about the vision, which leads to disengagement. An actively disengaged employee offers all sorts of resistance, most of it in the form of procrastinating and ignoring agreements. Unfortunately, disengagement runs rampant at work. In a 2022 Gallup poll, only 36 percent of US employees said they were engaged at work. That means that 64 percent are disengaged. The same study showed that 15 percent of US employees are *actively* disengaged at work, meaning that they are playing on social media, texting with friends, or looking for another job while on the payroll.

Disengaged employees probably won't cause overt conflict, because they don't care enough. But they do create dissatisfaction within the team, because they aren't pulling their weight, creating more work for everyone else. If disengagement drifts into overt resistance, overcome it by welcoming and playing dumb.

The resistance buster necessary for disengaged employees is reengagement. Reengagement comes from a variety of factors, but according to a 2019 Gallup poll, the common thread was maintaining a dialogue between leaders, managers, and employees. The poll showed that organizational cultures that held people accountable, had transparent communication, and focused on coaching rather than correcting saw dramatic increases in engagement. The content of the company communication and coaching process all had to do with personal development in regards to the company's vision.

All team members get disengaged periodically. As a project progresses, it's easy to lose sight of the vision and forget the *why*. Time is the enemy of engagement. The daily routine sucks excitement from a project and leaves even the most supportive team members bored and unfulfilled. Reminding everyone of the vision invigorates excitement and gets people back on track.

When reiterating the vision, have some fun with it! For team members who are already disengaged, reading the vision statement at a staff meeting hardly feels riveting. Having the vision statement spelled out in cupcakes, however, catches their attention. I had a client who assigned a different team member to creatively engage with the vision each month. One staff member sang it, another incorporated it into artwork, and another baked the cupcakes. See how you can get the team involved with the vision.

As you get team members involved with the vision, highlight how the skills they are using on this project can transfer to other areas of their careers. Help them recognize that staying engaged with the vision not only benefits the organization, but also their long-term goals.

Turning Resistance into Solutions

Instead of treating resistance like an obstacle, make it an opportunity. Use it as a chance to solicit input from team members. For example, when you encounter someone who gives a lot of excuses, use it as a learning tool. Have a courageous conversation and see if you can ascertain what is causing the disengagement. Can you learn anything from the excuse? Ask that person what would have helped them do better. The more you get productive input from team members, the more likely they are to take ownership and keep agreements. It's hard to be disengaged from something you helped create. You don't have to implement every suggestion, but soliciting input allows ideas to flow and fosters a culture of engagement. When your team is engaged, they rarely resist.

A common way to solicit input is to ask team members to bring a solution with them before they approach you with a problem. Leaders have used this strategy for decades to decrease the number of complaints. Thinking through potential solutions forces team members to take a broader view. Sometimes, just mulling over potential solutions makes a complaint disappear before it even gets to you. Expand on the idea and create a "solution session," which is the opposite of a bitch session. Anyone can participate and complain about whatever they want as long as he or she provides a solution. These sessions frequently turn into productive brainstorming meetings and become outlets for dissolving resistance.

How Harriet Tubman Overcame Resistance

One of the most dramatic examples of overcoming resistance without conflict was abolitionist Harriet Tubman. Tubman not only escaped slavery herself but made thirteen trips back into the pre–Civil War South to rescue other enslaved people, earning her the moniker "Moses." Bringing passengers on the dangerous trip along the Underground Railroad, Tubman encountered plenty of resistance. Despite her passengers' desire for freedom, their fear often kept them from keeping agreements on the journey. Tubman knew that one person's resistance could jeopardize the lives of all of her passengers, so she became masterful at overcoming resistance without drama or conflict.

Tubman was born into slavery in approximately 1822 in Dorchester County, Maryland. She was separated from her family at age five and hired out to masters who repeatedly beat and whipped her. At approximately age twelve, she suffered a traumatic head injury when the metal handle of a bullwhip hit her in the forehead. The injury caused dizziness, pain, and spells of hypersomnia for the rest of her life. The injury also corresponded with the onset of visions and vivid dreams, which Tubman ascribed to premonitions from God.

In 1849, Tubman escaped from slavery in Maryland to freedom in Philadelphia. Once in the North, she realized her freedom felt empty if her family wasn't also free. Within a year, the federal government passed the 1850 Fugitive Slave Act, which required that escaped slaves be returned to their owners. This jeopardized her freedom. It was no longer enough to live in a free state. Fugitives now had to go to Canada. Her loneliness and fear for her family compelled her to risk her own life and freedom to travel back to the South and bring enslaved people to Ontario. She claimed that in those trips, she "never lost a passenger" on the Underground Railroad.

Because of the extreme danger of her journeys, Tubman enforced strict agreements among all passengers. If a passenger agreed to come with her, that person followed Tubman's rules to the letter. She traveled in the winter, when nights were long and most people were inside. The group slept by day and moved at night. She always left on a Saturday night, since runaway slave notices weren't printed in the newspaper until Monday afternoon.

Tubman's hatred of slavery and commitment to ending it helped reframe any personal resistance she may have had. She must have been frightened for her own safety, especially as the bounty offered for her by Southern slaveholders increased to over $12,000 (equivalent to approximately $450,000 in 2020 dollars). Nevertheless, she shifted her mindset and let go of any resentment. She was never known to get angry. She approached every situation with curiosity, frequently wondering aloud how God would help her this time.

Tubman's childhood visions continued into adulthood, which she attributed to divine guidance.

Sometimes this presence gave her instructions that seemed counterintuitive, but she required the group do exactly as she said, even if it didn't make sense. In one example, she insisted that the group double back toward the plantation they just left. Some of the passengers grumbled, but Tubman demanded they stay together and do as they were told. Within minutes, slave catchers crossed the intersection to the north of them. If Tubman's passengers had continued on their original path, they would have been caught. Tubman's premonition saved the group.

Tubman carried a revolver and was not afraid to use it. She knew it provided some protection from slave catchers, but she also found it handy for overcoming resistance. Tubman threatened to shoot anyone who threatened the safety of her passengers. Tubman made everyone agree at the outset that if they started with her, they finished the trip. In one instance, a man got scared partway through the journey and decided to go back to the plantation. Tubman held the gun to his head and said, "You go on, or you die." He went and was with the group several days later when they reached southern Canada.

Tubman succeeded because she could welcome resistance with kind firmness. She had done the journey herself, so she understood the fear her passengers felt and never blamed them for their uncertainty. At the same time, she knew that anger wouldn't move them to freedom, so she refused to indulge in it. When they brought up resistance, she "played dumb" (if you can call threatening to shoot someone playing dumb) and insisted they move on. She talked about the joys of freedom whenever they had time to rest, to keep them engaged in the vision. There was no conflict in her group, because she knew that fighting among themselves would jeopardize the whole journey. By the time of the Civil War, Tubman had rescued more than 100 people from slavery.

Handling a Resistant Salesperson

No one's experience can match Tubman's for drama and impact, but you'll be more likely to relate to overcoming resistance in a business context, as Marissa did. A sales manager for a media outlet, she managed a team of salespeople responsible for selling print advertising in a monthly publication. During Marissa's tenure, print media was struggling, with many publications switching to online formats. Although several of her salespeople continued to get results, her top performer struggled. He missed quotas and started losing customers. The first time she talked to him, he gave her several excuses, claiming that the industry was changing and that his clients were no

longer advertising in print. Marissa felt herself getting annoyed at the excuses, so she gave him a quick
pep talk and ended the meeting.

The following month, however, his sales continued to decline. Worse, while traveling, Marissa picked
up a competing magazine at an airport newsstand and
saw a full-page ad for one of his customers that was
supposedly no longer purchasing print advertising.
Her initial reaction was to get angry and frustrated.
For the entire plane ride home, Marissa mentally
blamed and criticized him. Upon landing, she sent off
a quick email scheduling a check-in session on Monday morning.

Over the weekend, however, Marissa knew that if
she walked into the meeting angry, nothing productive would happen. She took the time to reframe the
conversation in her head and let go of blaming him.
She worked to approach Monday's conversation with
curiosity about his viewpoint on the industry. She
also thought of questions that would lead to an effective outcome. She practiced identifying her anger
cues and taking deep breaths to calm down.

When Monday came, Marissa started the meeting
by asking questions. She asked how sales had been.
She found herself genuinely curious, so she asked her
associate why he felt that the market was declining.
He gave the usual excuses about tight budgets, fear

of a recession, and publications moving online. She then showed him the full-page ad his former client took out in a rival publication, and instead of blaming him, simply asked why he thought they were no longer spending money on print advertising. She played dumb when the excuses came, continuing to reiterate the obvious fact that this client was buying print advertising. He offered a few more excuses, and Marissa said nothing.

When it was clear that he was running out of steam, Marissa reengaged him. She reminded him of their publication's vision and why it offered a benefit to advertisers. She instructed him to contact his client list and continue to offer them the value that they'd always received, and if they weren't buying, he was to ask why. He objected, and Marissa listened carefully to his objections, then played dumb again. She agreed that all of his concerns *might* happen, and then told him to make the calls anyway. After fifteen minutes of resistance, he exhausted his excuses and left the office, agreeing to make the calls.

She watched as he was reengaged over the course of the next month. She was concerned that his declining performance and resistance might be signs of disengagement, but he made the sales calls as promised, even if he lacked some of his old enthusiasm.

Whenever she could, she stopped by his office to casually chat about the magazine's vision. At the next month's meeting, Marissa was pleased to see that this gentleman was back in the top three salespeople. Although he still wasn't number one, his sales increased modestly, and he was getting results. He remained one of the top salespeople for several more years.

Although resistance is part of the human condition, you don't have to push back. You can easily overcome resistance by reframing the conversation in your own mind, welcoming resistance, playing dumb, and reengaging your team with the vision. Take the opportunity to turn resistance into solutions, and watch conflict evaporate.

Mindset Shifts

1. Learn to be aware of how resistance feels in your body. Can you notice when it arrives? What can you do to release it?
2. Let go of the idea that anyone is right or anyone is wrong.
3. Don't get angry.
4. Approach everything with curiosity.
5. Practice combining kindness with firmness.

New Habits

1. Take time each day to ascertain what resistance you might have. Use a journal if it's helpful.
2. Try welcoming resistance. When you feel yourself start to resist, try opening your arms and saying, "Welcome. Let's get through this!"
3. Practice playing dumb. Create a catchphrase suitable for the situation and use it repeatedly.
4. Learn how to say what you mean without getting angry.
5. Find new and creative ways to keep the vision front and center with your team.

6

END UNPRODUCTIVE RELATIONSHIPS PRODUCTIVELY

No matter how well you've anticipated problems, set expectations, held people accountable, and overcome resistance, there come times when relationships must end. If you're lucky, the other person will end it first. However, as a leader, you can't keep an unproductive relationship simply because you don't want to be a bitch. In personal relationships, I have known women who were rude to their boyfriends for months, hoping they would initiate the breakup. In professional relationships, I have watched bosses beg unproductive employees to stay simply because they didn't have anyone else to do the work. Unfortunately, part of leadership is periodically ending professional relationships and planning accordingly. In short, sometimes you must fire someone.

Leaders avoid conflict as much as anyone, which is most evident when a leader needs to let someone go. It's never easy, and many leaders wait until they're angry to do it. In a typical scenario, the leader talks to the person about a transgression, blames the employee for doing something wrong, and then dismisses that person in a cloud of shame. Alternately, the leader might blame the employee, then allow them to argue, defend, and accuse. The argument doesn't change the outcome. The end result is an antagonistic interchange in which neither party feels heard or respected.

There *is* a different way to do it. If you allow the cerebral cortex to override anger, the interaction can remain calm. In one instance where I had to let someone go, I pointed out everything this person did right, the things that weren't working (without laying blame), and said that I released him to go find something that better fit his skills and interests. I could have recited a laundry list of mistakes, botched interactions, and dropped balls. Instead, I declined to justify my decision, never got angry, and calmly executed my plan.

Within two months, this man found another position that better suited his talents. Meanwhile my organization implemented a restructure that allowed for more efficient job descriptions, increased pay for remaining staff members, and created financial savings in the annual budget. Everybody won, with minimal unpleasantness.

Not every challenge means that it's time to fire a team member. There are many stories about marginal employees who have turned around and become invaluable. I am a living example of that. In my first job out of college, I was incredibly insecure and uncertain about what I was doing. Unfortunately, this appeared to others as standoffishness and unwillingness to be a team player.

Luckily, I had a boss who believed in me. She took me aside and kindly told me how other people perceived me. I was mortified by how I'd come across and was eager to do whatever it took to prove to my colleagues that I wasn't really like that. My boss helped me keep agreements and meet expectations and held me accountable. I became one of the top employees, and in a short time worked my way into a management position. The moral of the story is, don't end the relationship at the first inkling of trouble.

On the other hand, don't take heroic measures to fix a problem situation. Professional relationships shouldn't be hard. How much you should do to fix a relationship? Not much. If the effort to manage a team member is greater than the return on your time investment, the relationship has become unproductive. If you have tried every strategy in this book and still feel conflict bubbling under the surface with a particular person, it's time to end the relationship.

How do you end the relationship so that you don't hurt morale or launch a mass exodus of good, productive employees? How do you fire someone without being a bitch?

Is It Really Over?

First, be sure the relationship is beyond repair. A straightforward definition of an unproductive professional relationship is one that no longer meets the objectives of the situation. For example, a colleague may have a lot of good qualities, but if this person isn't getting the desired results, the relationship has become unproductive. Similarly, a person may get everything done but has a toxic attitude and contributes to a bitter work culture. This is not the desired result either.

Relationships that are beyond repair tend to have some things in common. Such team members make the same mistakes over and over. They have a terrible attitude. They aren't receptive to feedback. No matter how much you've mastered conflict, these folks seem to breed it. They might be antagonistic. Check the steps from this book. Do you have agreements? Are the expectations clear? Have you held people accountable? Did you implement resistance busters? If you've tried all these strategies and a team member still isn't contributing, the relationship is beyond repair, and it's time to act.

It's hard to see at the time, but ending an unproductive relationship can be the most productive thing to do. It's also the greatest challenge you will face as a leader. Letting someone go feels like the ultimate conflict. Regardless of how long you've been a leader or how many times you've done it, firing someone always affects you profoundly. It's vital to your well-being and the outcome of the situation to make sure you are mentally prepared before you take action.

Prepare to Let Go

Before ending an unproductive relationship, check in with yourself. Evaluate your attitude toward the person and situation and see if you might be exaggerating the problem. Do you have preconceived notions about the person based on a single interaction? If so, can you verify that they're true? Also, identify your attitude. Don't assume that someone is doing a bad job until you've had a chance to talk to that person directly. It's also helpful to get outside feedback so you catch any biases you might have.

Release any sense of guilt, loss, or grief about ending the relationship. Let go of the idea that you are doing anything *to* the other person. Remember, this person has 100 percent responsibility for failing to keep agreements, meet expectations, and accept accountability. You are simply releasing this person to find a situation that aligns more closely with his or her talents. Process whatever emotions you have about the situation before you enter it. Don't let your limbic brain override your judgment or cause an inappropriate reaction during the critical meeting.

Although no one wants to be let go, this team member isn't happy, or else the relationship would still be productive. Remind yourself that your most important commitments are to yourself, the organization, and the rest of the team. Removing someone who isn't performing is a huge service to the people who are counting on you to lead them.

As you review why you're taking action, check your intentions. Be sure you are doing this for the highest good of everyone involved, not as retaliation. Sometimes, if a work relationship has been stressful for a while, it's easy to fool yourself about your reasons. You may want to end the relationship just to avoid having to deal with the other person. This isn't the best of intentions. Be clear about your motivation before acting.

Next, make sure your decision is based on respect for the other person. Unless someone has done something egregious, it's best to end the relationship respectfully. Just because the other person is struggling with some performance issue doesn't make him or her a bad person. It probably won't be your first impulse to think about all the good things in the person you're firing, but by focusing on good qualities, you release the person graciously. Let go of the need to be right or blame the person. In this situation, what does you gain? Nothing. It only keeps you from treating the other person civilly.

Prepare yourself for the other person's reaction. No matter how respectful you are, they probably won't react well. They may get defensive or lose control, and you will have to curtail the impulse to argue or defend yourself in return. They are backed into a corner and probably a little desperate, so they will make you the villain. Don't react to anything, and don't take it personally. You have the authority to end the relationship, so don't waste your leadership capital fighting an argument that doesn't matter. Mentally prepare yourself for the person to lash out, and never let yourself respond.

Finally, find the courage to follow through. This person may be angry, yell at you, call you names, maybe even threaten you, but stick to your guns. It's similar to playing dumb: your role isn't to convince this person of the wisdom or righteousness of your decision. Your role is to deliver the news and end the relationship without losing your cool, treating the other person with dignity and respect. You will probably trigger unresolved emotions in the other person—most of which have nothing to do with you. If the team member acts out, just stay calm. Your demeanor defines whether you ended the relationship productively or not.

No matter the reason for ending the relationship, it's never wise to burn bridges. The person you're letting go is a human being, processing a difficult situation. Don't throw gasoline onto the fire by arguing or belittling. You never know when you might meet this person again in a professional setting. If you've ended the relationship productively, you are ahead of the game in reestablishing the relationship as necessary. You are also gaining the respect of your remaining team members. Although the process is supposed to be confidential, word will get out about your interaction. Handle it in a way you would be proud for the rest of your team to know.

Ultimately, you can't control how the other person reacts. You can only control yourself. Be sure you handle things as well as you possibly can. Whether you ever see the other person again or not, maintain a reputation as a fair, calm, and compassionate leader rather than a tyrant. The way you handle this situation will model to your team how to have the ultimate courageous conversation. You will gain respect and loyalty by having the courage to end this unproductive relationship productively.

Logistics

After you've mentally prepared yourself to let someone go, there are a variety of logistical considerations. Definitely make a plan. Don't find yourself in the position of flying off the handle, losing your temper, and firing someone without thinking it through. If you're tempted to do this, take it as confirmation that you're in an unproductive relationship, but walk out of the room, take some deep breaths, and calm down so that you figure out next steps.

First, look at the roles and responsibilities that this person performs. Is there any built-in redundancy? Is there someone else who can step in and take over? Make sure you know everything this person does, so you don't find yourself with something uncovered later. You don't want to end the relationship only to create more work for team members who are engaged and productive.

Second, decide who should know about this change ahead of time. The list of people should be very short, but sometimes you need to prepare someone for the change before you let a person go. I once made the mistake of terminating a person's position without telling his assistant. She learned of the decision in the staff meeting with everyone else. She was so devoted to the person I let go that she broke down in the staff meeting and was then embarrassed by her intense reaction. Because of confidentiality, I didn't tell her before it happened, but in hindsight, I should have talked to her privately immediately before announcing to the entire staff.

If you are lucky enough to have a human resources (HR) department, the third step is to talk to someone in that department about the requirements. There will be paperwork to sign, paid time off to sort out, and legalities to think about. You don't want to do this on impulse. Have everything you need ready to go before you actually do anything. Have a witness present when you end the relationship, and follow all HR protocols and policies.

Fourth, document, document, document! Include a good time line of events that caused problems, a record of behavior that was unacceptable, and a clear understanding of how this negatively impacted your team, project, or organization. Check with your HR staff member so you have the documents you need legally. They must be clear, concise, and compassionate. Explain your decision; make sure you are transparent about how you made it and why.

Finally, practice what you're going to say. Don't wing this! If you have been tempted in a fit of rage to fire this person before, it is imperative to practice what you're going to say so you stay calm and keep your temper in check. Similarly, practice so you don't back down. Ask your spouse or a friend outside of work to role-play with you. Pro tip: if your spouse or friend can be *especially* unpleasant and petulant, it will set you up for success by allowing you to think about every eventuality and be ready with a response for a wide variety of arguments. The better prepared you are, the less of a bitch you're likely to be while managing this ultimate conflict.

Good Stuff on the Other Side

Leaders tend to dread ending unproductive relationships because they are focused on the unpleasantness of the actual interaction instead of seeing the good stuff on the other side.

Try this. Make a fist. Now take that fist and, without opening it, attempt to pick up a handful of something you want—M&Ms, potato chips, coins, or something else. You can't do it, can you? Of course not! That's just ridiculous! You've closed off the mechanism by which you can acquire what you want. It is just common sense.

It's harder to see it that way with professional relationships. If you get distracted from ending an unproductive relationship because you're afraid of the potential conflict, you lose sight of what you actually want. Your goal is a functioning team. Stay focused on the productive, synergistic, results-oriented workplace you desire. If you try to make the wrong person fit while going for a big goal, it's like trying to dip into that yummy bowl of M&Ms with a closed fist. Having a team member who fits your objectives means letting go of one who doesn't. Nothing hurts morale more than watching a leader work around one intransigent or difficult person rather than ending the relationship and having a person who really fits.

If you end an unproductive relationship productively, not only will you have removed a problem who was draining time and energy from your team, but you will also have opened the door to attract people who are more aligned with your vision, more engaged with your project, and more excited about what you are trying to do. You will find new team members to step into leadership, and the entire team will begin to embrace opportunities.

You and your team will find the good stuff, but so will the person you let go. If the relationship has become unproductive, the other person will be as glad to be gone as you are to have them gone. Usually someone who isn't performing well is just hanging on because of fear about finding another job. If you force the situation, the person has to move on and almost always finds something better. I have never yet let someone go who didn't end up with a better opportunity, whether it was a job that was a better fit, the chance to start their own business, or the ability to stay home with family.

Seeing the good stuff on the other side entails keeping the big picture in mind. Remember, your organization's vision is bigger than any individual team member—even you. As a leader, your job is to be a steward of the organization's resources and vision. Focusing on the discomfort of ending a relationship misses the point of building an effective team. If you allow one person's agenda to dictate how you run the team, you are looking too closely at the day-to-day operations and missing the opportunity to enhance your leadership in attaining the vision.

Eleanor Roosevelt and the DAR

One of the best examples of ending an unproductive relationship productively comes from Eleanor Roosevelt, one of my role models. In 1939, Roosevelt publicly ended an unproductive relationship in a way that was so productive, it advanced civil rights in the United States and led to substantive policy changes. That year, the president of Howard University in Washington, D.C., invited famed contralto opera singer Marian Anderson to perform. Anderson, an African American, had headlined an annual concert at Howard every year since 1936, and each year the crowds grew. By 1939, the university needed a larger venue.

Howard University's president petitioned the Daughters of the American Revolution (DAR), a patriotic organization, to use its auditorium, Constitution Hall, for a concert on Easter weekend. The hall was the largest venue in the city, holding over 4,000 people. However, in 1939, Washington was still segregated, and the DAR practiced an aggressive form of "patriotism" that included an all-white agenda. Although the organizers of the concert hoped that Anderson's worldwide fame and reputation would encourage the DAR to make an exception to its restrictive policy, the DAR declined the request.

First lady Eleanor Roosevelt watched this exchange with interest, although she didn't get involved immediately. She had been given membership in the DAR when she became first lady but was not an active member. She initially didn't weigh in on the situation: she believed it was so bad that other people who had more influence with the DAR would certainly protest. But none of them felt they had the power to instigate change.

When no protests were forthcoming, Roosevelt looked for signs that the relationship was beyond repair. She first tried to make members of the DAR accountable by attending and organizing high-profile events with Anderson. Roosevelt agreed to make an appearance to present the Springarn Medal (for outstanding achievement by an African American) to Anderson at the national convention of the National Association for the Advancement of Colored People (NAACP). She invited Anderson to perform at the White House for the king and queen of England. With each action, she signaled her vision for civil equality, believing the DAR must share the same vision. She hoped the DAR would relent on its policy, or at least more active members of the DAR would challenge the group's policy.

When Roosevelt's subtle tactics didn't work, she realized she would have to take direct action.

In February 1939, Roosevelt submitted her letter of resignation to the DAR president, declaring that the organization had "set an example which seems to me unfortunate" and that the DAR had "an opportunity to lead in an enlightened way" but had "failed to do so." Roosevelt wrote about the issue in her newspaper column, which was published across the country. Out of respect for the DAR, she didn't mention either the organization or Anderson by name, although she talked about her struggle with the decision to resign or try to initiate change from within. She finally concluded that "to remain as a member implies approval of that action, therefore I am resigning."

In addition to ending her relationship with the DAR, Roosevelt created the good stuff on the other side. She worked with secretary of the interior Harold Ickes to secure the Lincoln Memorial as the site of the Easter concert featuring Anderson. She lobbied every radio network to broadcast the concert live. Consequently, instead of playing at Constitution Hall for an audience of 4,000 people, Roosevelt ensured that Anderson's concert could be attended by 75,000 people of all ages, races, and religions. It was also broadcast to hundreds of thousands over the radio. Roosevelt declined to attend so as not to distract attention from Anderson. Secretary Ickes, acting as master of ceremonies, addressed Roosevelt's vision when he introduced Anderson, saying, "Genius knows no color line."

When ending her unproductive relationship with the Daughters of the American Revolution, Eleanor Roosevelt took her time in relinquishing her membership to make sure her intentions were pure. She ended the relationship with respect. She then created and embraced the good stuff on the other side. Although the DAR didn't desegregate Constitution Hall until 1953, Roosevelt created a watershed moment in American civil rights history, bringing national attention to the color barrier as no previous event had.

Dealing with Two at Once

Following Roosevelt's example, I had a situation where I ended not one, but two, unproductive relationships at the same time. I supervised a manager and an assistant manager who ran a department together but could not get along. If one made a decision, the other undermined it. Team members were constantly affected by the tension and felt pulled between the two managers. Every week, one of the managers was in my office complaining about the other one. Just when I thought I had identified which relationship was unproductive, the other manager would come to me with an outrageous story about the first one, and I hesitated. I realized something had to change, but I wasn't sure which one needed to go.

Finally, I spent a lot of money to have a high-level leadership coach do a weekend retreat with the team. I held both these employees accountable and told them, in front of the team, that the blaming and sniping would no longer be tolerated. I carefully outlined the behavior I expected. We all signed an agreement claiming we would give our coworkers the benefit of the doubt and ask questions rather than complain about each other. I left Sunday afternoon believing I had finally solved the problem.

Before noon on Monday, both managers called me to complain that the other one wasn't keeping the commitment. That's when I realized that I had not one, but *two* unproductive relationships. I had to fire them both. First, I mentally prepared myself. I was clear about my desired outcome and made sure I had the best of intentions. I reminded myself of how much I respected both of them for their work. I let go of any preconceived notions I had about either person and worked to think of them both with love and respect.

Next, I summoned all my courage. Both of these managers had been friends of mine before we became coworkers. I did not relish the task in front of me, but I reminded myself that my first responsibility was to the team and the organization. I also knew that both managers had other friends in the organization, and I was going to be vilified for a few weeks until things settled down. I made sure I was prepared to treat both of them with respect. I practiced multiple times with my husband, who threw plenty of nasty comebacks at me. (I think he actually enjoyed it.) I was mentally prepared to let them go.

I implemented the logistical steps. Because I was releasing two managers, not one, it took some creativity to find redundancy and prepare the team, but within a month, I was ready. I met with HR, filed all the documents, and arranged to have a witness present. I let them go the same day. I knew I made the right decision because they both seemed shocked that it was happening and couldn't understand what the problem was. At that point, I was certain these relationships were beyond repair.

Almost immediately, we found the good stuff on the other side. Our team became functional, our projects moved forward, and we all pulled in the same direction. The organization ran better than ever, and new people stepped into leadership roles, bringing creativity and fresh perspectives to our work. Moreover, the people I let go were both happier. They each found jobs that suited them better and ended up having more fulfilling careers. My only regret was that I waited so long to end the unproductive relationships. Had I been less worried about the uncomfortable conversation and more invested in the big picture, we could have gotten to the good stuff on the other side a year earlier.

The point here is that you don't need to go to great lengths to have productive relationships. If your vision is aligned and everyone is engaged, it should be simple. Most importantly, you'll find that you have mastered the biggest fear of most leaders—the conflict potentially involved in letting someone go. If you do it productively, you will have gained respect from your team, left the overall relationship intact with the person you are releasing, and done it all without having to resort to being a bitch.

Mindset Shifts

1. Be clear about what you want from your professional relationships.
2. Mentally prepare yourself to end an unproductive relationship by making sure you're doing it with the best of intentions.
3. Approach the person you're letting go with respect.
4. Remind yourself of your responsibility to the organization and the remaining team members.
5. Imagine the good stuff on the other side of the uncomfortable conversation.

New Habits

1. Find the unproductive relationships on your team. How will you handle them?
2. Think of a negative situation. Now write three good things that could come from ending it.
3. Know your HR policy for ending professional relationships.
4. Create a succession plan for key positions.
5. Find someone willing to practice the conversation of ending an unproductive relationship. Urge them to be nasty and petulant.

7

CONCLUSION

Although you may not love conflict more now than you did when you started this book, hopefully you at least are more comfortable with it. I have introduced five strategies to help you navigate conflict without being a bitch. Although I've outlined each strategy in separate chapters, they frequently overlap and blend together, depending on your situation. As long as you master the skills in each chapter, they collectively provide a set of emotional tools to take into any situation and feel confident that you will get results without losing your cool.

First, anticipate potential conflicts. Build your emotional intelligence so you have self-awareness, self-management, social awareness, and relationship management skills. Never take anything personally.

Learn to identify emotional triggers in yourself, and have strategies in place to defuse them.

Armed with your own emotional intelligence, establish agreements among team members. Build on shared values so you have a common foundation. Assess the level of trust between individuals and groups, and listen actively to catch problems before they arise. Introduce the practice of the premortem so you can get the team involved in anticipating conflict. Then establish benchmarks. This allows you to manage behaviors that slow progress on the project and accept civil disagreements that don't threaten the team. There's no need to waste time defusing disagreements that don't affect you.

Second, set clear expectations. Start by determining realistic guidelines for yourself. Know your strengths, your limitations, and your boundaries. Find your Zone of Genius, and operate from there. Once you are clear about yourself, practice that same clarity with your team. Communicate as transparently as possible. Educate the entire team about your vision, and assign a workload, answering all of the question words. Include a time line. Summarize assignments, and have team members repeat them back so you know they've understood. These expectations are built on the agreements you made with your team and inform how the group works together.

Third, get comfortable holding people accountable. Identify any personal missteps and accept responsibility. Apologize as necessary. Then practice having courageous conversations. Approach the situation with empathy, and avoid rushing to blame. Ask questions to be sure you understand the situation. Don't assume anything. Tell the truth about the problem, and don't dance around the situation. Be direct and kind. Coach rather than correct. Don't dwell on the problems of the past. Stay focused on the desired outcome for the future.

Fourth, learn to overcome resistance in both you and your team. Reframe your internal conversation to defuse any personal resistance you may have. Practice approaching topics with curiosity. Anticipate the excuses you'll get and be ready to address them. Avoid getting angry: it robs you of your power and puts the other person on the defensive, which invites conflict. Learn the art of welcoming resistance with kind firmness. If the other person wants to argue, play dumb. (It works every time.) Turn resistance into solutions by engaging the other person with the vision and soliciting input from the team.

Finally, don't be afraid to end unproductive relationships. It's possible to do it productively. Assess your willingness to fix the relationship, and look for signs that it is beyond repair. Mentally prepare yourself to let the employee go, and have good intentions when you do. Find reasons to respect the other person, and summon the courage to end things respectfully. There is no need to get nasty. Remember, you want to stay high-minded throughout the process. Address the practical considerations in ending the relationship, and keep focused on the good stuff on the other side. You can't have the outstanding work relationship you really want while trying to cling to the unproductive relationships you don't.

You've probably noticed that each of these concepts begins with you. It's easy to believe that conflict is about the other people in your life, but that is almost never true. As the old saying goes, "It takes two to tango." No one can have conflict alone. Once you practice the mindset shifts and new behaviors at the end of each chapter, you can maintain your personal peace in any situation.

If you master all of these techniques, conflict will no longer be part of your reality. You don't have to love it, but you'll know you can navigate it. Your goal isn't to instigate it or go looking for it, but you shouldn't have to waste precious time and energy avoiding it either. When you are clear, firm, direct, and transparent, you can handle any conflict without being a bitch.

ACKNOWLEDGMENTS

Conflict is one of the most misunderstood of all human interactions. My fascination with conflict began as a child and has continued through all my professional endeavors. In my decades of trying to avoid it, I became an unwitting student of it, and there are several people I want to thank for helping me on the journey.

First, I want to thank all of the people in my life who have been conflict-avoidant. You know who you are. Ex-husbands, current and former friends, family members, and colleagues taught me how to handle conflict with kid gloves. Thank you for forcing me to be kind while getting my way.

Second, I am grateful to the women leaders who have served as my role models. I have watched them navigate conflict and sometimes ruin their reputations to be effective as females in positions of power. Thanks especially to Kathy Hearn, Michelle Medrano, Cynthia James, Virginia Scharff, and Sandy Emmert. You may not have known I was watching, but you taught me immeasurably.

Third, I want to thank Makayla Shirley, the coach who forced me to get clear on what I wanted to say. By hounding me into a fit of frustration, you gave me the title and outline for this book in a fifteen-minute conversation.

Finally, I want to thank my daughter, Kinsey Matetich, and my stepdaughter, Cleo Burton. You two are the reason I am so passionate about teaching women how to be powerful, authentic, and kind leaders. You are both perfect examples of that model.

ABOUT THE AUTHOR

Dr. Judy Morley is a nationally recognized business speaker and coach whose primary topics include conscious business, purposeful leadership, and emotional intelligence. Her main focus is to help entrepreneurs and business owners lead purposefully, authentically, and audaciously.

Her years of experience vary from being an advertising agency owner to a college professor to an executive to an entrepreneur and restaurant chain owner. She is even an ordained minister. Each of these positions has given her great insight into helping people find their authentic style of leadership.

Dr. Morley holds a PhD in American History and a master's degree in Conscious Leadership, as well as being a certified Emotional Intelligence facilitator.

She is the author of more than a dozen essays and books, including *5 Spiritual Steps to Overcome Adversity: Use the Cosmic 2x4 to Hit a Home Run*, and *The Leadership Constant: Audacious Strategies for Navigating Change.* She has been featured in several documentaries, including *MPower: Empowering Women in Business and Beyond.*

Dr. Morley is on the faculty of the Lincoln Leadership Institute at Gettysburg and serves a president of You Do You Coaching, a leadership coaching firm located in Gettysburg, Pennsylvania.

She and her husband are the founders and owners of Tilford's Wood Fired Pizza, with locations in several states, and SavorHood, a food hall and eatery in Gettysburg.

You can connect with Dr. Morley online via Facebook, Instagram, or at www.drjudymorley.net.

CPSIA information can be obtained
at www.ICGtesting.com
Printed in the USA
JSHW031246280123
36984JS00004B/5